Contents

Introduction

I am a process person: the making of something is as important to me as is the finished product. Watching something take shape is fascinating, and knowledge of the process adds to the beauty of the finished piece. I recently found myself mesmerized by a Saturday morning TV show on woodworking, on which Norm was demonstrating how to make a two-tiered louvered cupola. Although I have no woodworking experience and no place to put a cupola, I was glued to the TV for one entire hour.

Several years ago I worked as an artist at a small publishing company, drawing designs for cross stitch and needlepoint. After the designs were drawn on the grid paper, they were given to stitchers who transferred the artwork onto evenweave fabrics. With hundreds of floss colors to incorporate, a finished cross-stitch composition resembles a lovely painting. It was exciting and rewarding to see the completed creations.

The irony is that although I love the look of cross stitch, I don't enjoy cross stitching. Fortunately, we were not content in producing only needlework and we branched out into other popular crafting techniques, including quilting and appliqué. Bingo! I love the feel of fabric—cotton, flannel, silk, wool, and corduroy. I love combining fabrics. Only a quilter would describe mixing and matching colors, textures, and patterns as exhilarating. I love stitching the pieces together and watching the projects take shape. Sometimes the finished composition looks exactly as you imagined it would when you started. But occasionally you will surprise yourself and end up with something totally unexpected. Either way, you win.

This book was designed for fabric people who are also process people. These five new appliqué techniques are not only beautiful to look at; they're fun to do. The techniques differ from one another but each is unique and will add a new dimension to your fabric creations. Some techniques are based on art forms with which you may already be familiar, including paper cutting and yarn painting. I encourage you to search the Internet or the library to view authentic examples of the art forms from which these wonderful appliqué techniques have been derived.

The New Appliqué

Innovative Techniques, Easy Projects

Trice Boerens • *Photography by Kevin Dilley*

WATSON-GUPTILL PUBLICATIONS / NEW YORK

Senior Acquisitions Editor: Joy Aquilino

Edited by Amy Handy

Designed by Margo Mooney

Graphic production by Hector Campbell

Principal text type: New Century Schoolbook and Syntax

First published in 2004 by Watson-Guptill Publications,
a division of VNU Business Media, Inc.,
770 Broadway, New York, NY 10003
www.wgpub.com

ISBN 0-8230-3183-7

Library of Congress Control Number: 2004107255

Printed in the United States of America

First printing, 2004

1 2 3 4 5 6 7 8 9 / 12 11 10 09 08 07 06 05 04

General Instructions

All projects require a few very basic supplies that are not given in the materials lists: tracing paper for transferring patterns, a sewing machine, scissors, pins, and often a hand-sewing needle. Unless otherwise specified, fabric is cotton. When small pieces of fabric considerably less than ⅛ yard are needed, they are described in the materials lists as scraps. All measurements are given as width x length, except for those of strips used for borders, which are given as length x width. All projects are constructed with ¼-inch seam allowances. Materials lists for pillows include pillow forms or polyester fiberfill for stuffing. Pillow forms are more convenient to use and are suggested for standard-size projects. For pillows of unique size or shape, fiberfill is suggested. Many of the techniques require multiple rows or layers of machine stitching. Trim thread ends on the back and the front of the fabric often while working and again when the project is completed.

Transferring Patterns

Design templates are actual size whenever possible. If an enlargement is called for, photocopy the template at the specified enlargement percentage.

Note that instructions for transferring designs may vary according to technique. For example, some designs are to be drawn on the right side of the fabric and some are to be drawn on the wrong side. Also, required marking pens or pencils change according to project. Consult the chapter introductions for specific instructions.

Generally, patterns are transferred this way. First, trace the template onto tracing paper. Be as accurate as possible, especially with templates that are complex or small in scale. Next, carefully cut out the design along the marked lines. Finally, pin the template on the fabric and trace around the edge with marking pen or pencil.

Pinning and Basting

To secure two or more layers of fabric before stitching, use dressmaker's pins or basting stitches. Pinning is quicker, but be careful when stitching over pins. Place pins at a right angle to stitching line. Feed pins slowly under the presser foot to avoid hitting them with the needle, or remove them before they reach the presser foot. Basting stitches are large over/under running stitches inserted by hand. Use a contrasting thread color to make basting easy to see and to remove. Since these stitches are temporary, it is not necessary to knot the ends when starting and stopping.

Log Cabin Border

The Log Cabin is a classic quilt design. The assembly process shown in the diagram is adapted for a basic border.

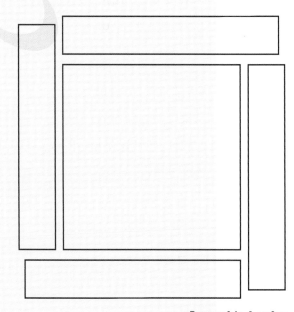

Log cabin border

Mitered Corners

When the corners of a border are mitered, or stitched diagonally, the border has the appearance of a picture frame. Stitch through adjoining ends at a 45-degree angle. Clip the seam at the intersection and press flat.

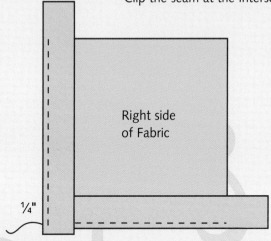

Right side of Fabric

¼"

Mitered corner, step 1

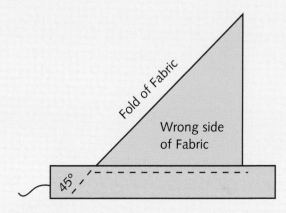

Fold of Fabric

Wrong side of Fabric

45°

Mitered corner, step 2

Machine Quilting

For a uniform quilting pattern, mark quilt top with an air-soluble marking pen before layering with batting and backing. There is no need to mark quilt top for a quilting pattern that follows the piecing pattern, or for parallel lines or freeform patterns.

Here are some quilting pointers:

❋ Work from the center out.

❋ Use both hands to secure the areas around the stitching lines.

❋ Stitch at a slower speed than that of normal sewing.

❋ Roll the quilt on the right edge as it accumulates under the machine.

Binding

Binding finishes the quilt edges quilt with a narrow, neat border. Trim batting and backing even with quilt top. Leave the first few inches of binding unattached. With raw edges even, stitch binding to quilt top. At corners, stop ¼ inch from edges. Fold binding at a right angle, turn quilt, realign raw edge of quilt with raw edge of binding, and continue stitching. When returning to the starting point, fold edge of lower binding end under and overlap opposite end. Fold binding around raw edge of quilt, and hand-stitch remaining folded edge of binding to back of quilt. At corners, tuck binding under for a diagonal fold.

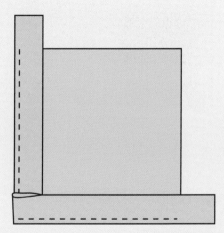

Binding

Facing

Facing finishes the quilt edges with no visible border. Trim batting and backing even with quilt top. For quilt sides, cut facing strips 3 to 4 inches wide and the same length as quilt. With right sides together and raw edges even, stitch strips to quilt sides. Press strips away from seam line, fold to back of quilt, and pin in place. Turn raw edge of facing under and hand-stitch it to quilt back.

For top and bottom of quilt, cut facing strips 3 inches longer than width of quilt. Center and stitch strips to top and bottom. Fold in ends of strips so they are flush with quilt sides. Press strips away from seam line, fold to back of quilt, and pin in place. Turn raw edge of facing under and hand-stitch it to quilt back.

Hand-Appliqué Shapes

To make a smooth, continuous edge for hand-appliqué shapes, face shape with lightweight fabric, such as organza, then follow these basic steps:

1. Machine stitch around entire perimeter of shape. **(See Photo A.)**

2. Trim around shape, clipping curves and cutting a single diagonal slit through the organza. **(See Photo B.)**

3. Turn right side out and press to hide organza on wrong side of shape. **(See Photo C.)**

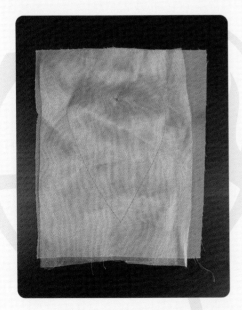

Photo A

Photo B

Photo C

Felt Layering

In simple terms, traditional appliqué entails stitching a fabric design on top of a background. Reverse appliqué means stitching layers of two or more pieces of fabric and cutting a design through the top layers to reveal the fabric or fabrics behind it. The raw edges are then turned under and stitched to the bottom layer.

Mola making is a remarkable art form practiced by the Kuna Indians of Panama. In this complex example of reverse applique, an individual piece may have as many as ten layers of fabric and can take up to one hundred hours to complete. Inspired by body painting, the stitched designs of people and animals include several rows of outlining around each figure. It's easy to get lost in mentally deconstructing the labyrinth of a mola's colored lines. Kuna societies take mola production very seriously. The entire community structure is built around it, with the young women stitching all day and the older women caring for the children and cooking. Using molas as springboards, this easy technique was born. The stitching is done with a sewing machine, eliminating tedious hand stitching. Since felt is the featured layering fiber, the cut edges will not fray nor unravel. Note that since the designs are applied on the wrong side of the fabric, all templates in this chapter are represented in mirror image, so trace them as they are. Although the process is stitched in several steps, draw the entire design before stitching.

The felt layering process also reminds me of scratchboard art, in which an illustration board is covered with a layer of white or rainbow paint, coated with black ink, and drawn on with a stylus. The black topcoat is thus scratched away to reveal the white or colored undercoat. At a quilt exhibit I observed an intriguing composition called, appropriately enough, "Scratch Board," made with a black top layer and a wild paisley print underneath. Trees and leaves were cut away to unveil a colorful spring landscape. Scratchboard is a fitting metaphor for reverse appliqué, with the design being uncovered with scissors rather than a stylus.

Basic Instructions: Simple Technique

The easy version, as represented in the **Bird** and **Autumn Quilts**, appears to be a fabric shape outlined with felt. It is completed in four steps:

1. Draw the design on the wrong side of the bottom layer of fabric **(see Photo A)**.

2. Layer the fabric and the felt. The layering sequence is critical. Since the stitching is done from the back, the sequence will be reversed when viewed from the front **(see Photo B)**.

3. Stitch on the wrong side of the fabric on the marked lines. When starting and stopping, reverse the direction for two or three stitches to prevent unraveling.

4. Trim the top layers—one fabric and one felt. It is easy to catch lower layers in the scissors by mistake, so be careful to trim through only the designated areas **(see Photos C, D)**.

Photo A

Photo B

Photo C

Photo D

A more complex version of reverse appliqué is used in constructing the tops for the Nest, Crocodile, and Fish Pillows, which utilize four or five layers of cotton fabric, felt, and cotton jersey. The cut edge of jersey is not as clean as that of felt but it resists fraying and works well in this process.

After stitching and trimming the first sequence of layers, one or two additional layers are added as *inlaid appliqué,* which refers to appliquéd details added to recessed areas. These details can be either secondary design elements or focal points. The number of layers is limited by the height between the floor of the sewing machine and the presser foot. If your machine will not accommodate the number of colors needed, inlaid areas can be added later.

At first glance the process may seem intimidating, but if the steps are followed carefully you will be successful. Note that each pillow has its own stitching sequence.

Basic Instructions: Inlaid Technique

1. Draw the entire design on the bottom layer of fabric **(see Photo E)**. Since the designs are more complex, it is easier to trace them directly onto lightweight cotton fabric rather than to transfer them with templates.

2. Layer the fabric and the felt for the background design **(see Photo F)**.

3. Stitch on the wrong side of the fabric on the marked lines. When starting and stopping, reverse the direction for two or three stitches to prevent unraveling.

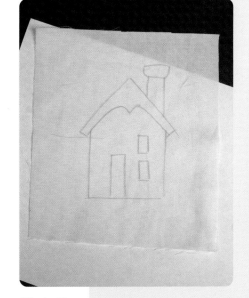

Photo E

Photo F

4. Trim the top three to four layers **(see Photos G, H, I)**.

5. Layer the inlaid areas for the accents.

6. Stitch from the back on the accents lines.

7. Trim the inlaid areas.

Helpful Hints

✳ Use a number 2 pencil or a colored pencil to draw the design. Since the design is drawn on the wrong side of the fabric the lines won't be visible from the front, but if you want them to disappear, use an air-soluble marking pen instead.

✳ Choose sharp scissors with a pointed end. In order to achieve accurate and detailed cuts, the cutting is done with the tips of the scissors rather than near the hinge.

✳ This technique requires that you think in reverse and use both sides of your brain, the analytical side as well as the creative side. Experiment by stitching on layered fabric with freeform scribble designs.

Photo I

Photo G

Photo H

Nest Pillow

As a bird will build a nest of humble materials like grass and twigs, this one is built with layers of ordinary polyester felt.

Materials

12-inch square lightweight white cotton

12-inch felt squares in camel, bronze, dark blue, medium blue, purple, tan, and cream

12-inch jersey squares in black and camel

½ yard cream-and-blue herringbone fabric

Four 1 x 13-inch strips purple felt

Black, light blue, and tan thread

14-inch pillow form

Marking pen or pencil

FINISHED SIZE
14 inches square

1. Prepare template on page 91 **(see Transferring Patterns, page 5)**. Trace design onto center of white fabric. Layer 12-inch squares on work surface in this order: bronze felt, black jersey, dark blue felt, camel jersey, and marked white fabric. Pin through all layers at corners. With black thread, stitch on black lines; remove pins. On right side of square, trim bronze felt on both sides of stitched lines. Trim black jersey and dark blue felt from inside corners to reveal camel jersey.

2. On wrong side of square, stitch on broken lines. Trim black jersey from inside sections 1 through 6 to reveal dark blue felt.

3. Place medium blue felt on work surface. Place layered square, wrong side up, on felt. Pin at corners. With light blue thread, stitch on blue lines; remove pins. On right side of square, trim medium blue felt on both sides of stitched lines.

4. Place purple felt on work surface. Place layered square, wrong side up, on felt. Pin at corners. Stitch on purple lines; remove pins. On right side of square, trim purple felt on both sides of stitched lines.

5. Place tan felt on work surface. Place layered square, wrong side up, on felt. Pin at corners. With tan thread, stitch on brown lines; remove pins. On right side of square, trim tan felt on both sides of stitched lines. Trim black jersey from inside feathers and nest to reveal dark blue felt. Trim dark blue felt from nest sections to reveal camel jersey.

6. Place cream felt on work surface. Place layered square, wrong side up, on felt. Pin at corners. Stitch on gray lines; remove pins. On right side of square, trim around eggs.

7. Using corner sections as guides, from medium blue felt cut irregular shapes to fit inside them. Adjust sewing machine to wide satin stitch, and with blue thread, stitch ¼-inch lines to secure felt in corners. Trim black jersey from around bronze felt border to reveal dark blue felt.

8. From herringbone fabric, cut 14½-inch square. Center and pin layered square to right side of herringbone square. With black thread, stitch around square ¼ inch from bronze felt border; remove pins. Trim around stitched square.

9. From herringbone fabric, cut second 14½-inch square. Place square, right side up, on work surface. Center and place purple felt strips on square, aligning strips with cut edges of square. Pin in place. With right sides together, pin square to pillow top. Stitch together, leaving 8-inch opening along one side; remove pins. Trim excess fabric from corners. Turn right side out. Insert pillow form. Hand stitch opening closed.

Crocodile Pillow

Introduce print fabrics to a composition of flat, mat felt, and make your family and friends grin along with this smiling croc and his fishy pals.

Materials

13½ x 12½-inch rectangles of lightweight white cotton, lime green felt, turquoise felt, tan felt, orange cotton jersey, and light blue felt

Scrap of yellow felt

¼ yard brown print fabric

⅛ yard green print fabric

⅛ yard dark green felt

Scrap of orange print fabric

Scraps of gold fabric

½ yard rust textured fabric

¼ yard fusible web

Dark green, tan, light blue, and yellow thread

Mixed yellow mini beads

Polyester fiberfill

Marking pen or pencil

Black fabric marking pen

Air-soluble marker

Double-sided adhesive, such as Peel-N-Stick™

FINISHED SIZE
16 x 15 inches

1. Prepare templates on pages 90 and 92 (see Transferring Patterns, page 5). Trace design onto center of white fabric. Layer 13½ x 12½-inch rectangles on work surface in this order: lime green felt, turquoise felt, tan felt, orange cotton jersey, and marked white fabric. Pin through all layers at corners. With green thread, stitch on black lines; remove pins. On right side of rectangle, trim lime green felt on both sides of stitched lines.

2. On wrong side, stitch along broken line. On right side, trim turquoise on both sides of stitched lines. Trim tan from outside edge of border to reveal orange. Trim felt from sections 1–12 to reveal orange.

3. From yellow felt, cut 4-inch square. With wrong side up, center brown corner triangle on felt. With yellow thread, stitch on brown line. On right side, trim around triangle. Repeat for remaining corner triangles.

4. Place light blue felt on work surface. Place stitched rectangle, wrong side up, on felt. With blue thread, stitch on blue line. On right side of rectangle, trim light blue felt from inside border to reveal layered design.

5. From green print, cut 7 x 5-inch rectangle. From dark green felt, cut 7 x 5-inch rectangle. Place felt on work surface. Place fabric, wrong side up, on felt. Center crocodile on layered fabrics. Pin through all layers at corners. Stitch on green lines; remove pins. On right side, trim felt and fabric from around crocodile. Trim felt inside crocodile to reveal green print.

6. Prepare background and fish templates. From brown print fabric, cut 7½ x 6-inch rectangle. From fusible web, cut 7½ x 6-inch rectangle. Following manufacturer's directions, fuse web to wrong side of background fabric. Draw background shape on paper side of fusible web and cut, including area inside tail. Fuse background to center of rectangle.

7. From orange print, cut 2-inch square. From fusible web, cut 2-inch square. Fuse web to wrong side of fabric. Draw a fish on paper side of fusible web and cut out. Referring to photo for placement, fuse fish to brown print. With gold fabric, make two more fish and fuse in place.

8. Adjust sewing machine to narrow zigzag with about 24 stitches per inch. With tan thread, stitch on outside edge of background shape and fish.

9. From double-sided adhesive, cut three 1½ x 1 x 1-inch triangles. Remove paper backing and, referring to photo for placement, press rectangles in place to adhere. Remove remaining paper and sprinkle beads on exposed adhesive. With fabric marking pen, draw eyes where indicated.

10. From rust fabric, cut two 16½ x 15½-inch rectangles. With air-soluble marker, draw 11 x 10-inch rectangle centered on light blue felt. Pin layered rectangle in center of right side of one rust rectangle. With blue thread, stitch on marked line. Trim around stitched rectangle. With right sides together, pin to second rust rectangle and stitch, leaving 6-inch opening along one side; remove pins. Trim excess fabric from corners. Turn right side out. Stuff with fiberfill. Hand-stitch opening closed.

Fish Pillow

The perfect gift for the fisherman or the faux fisherman in your life, this design is an interesting fish stew of geometric shapes rendered in vibrant colors.

Materials

12½ x 10-inch rectangles of lightweight white cotton, gold felt (two), black felt (two), purple felt, blue plaid fabric, and green felt

Scraps of pink velvet and orange felt

12½ x 3-inch strips of turquoise, black, and light blue felt

½ yard blue print fabric

Purple thread

Black embroidery floss

Polyester fiberfill

Marking pen or pencil

FINISHED SIZE
16 x 12 inches

1. Prepare template on page 96 **(see Transferring Patterns, page 5)**. Trace design in center of white fabric. Layer 12½ x 10-inch rectangles on work surface in this order: gold felt, black felt, purple felt, black felt, blue plaid, and marked white fabric. Pin through all layers at corners. Stitch on black lines; remove pins. On right side, trim gold felt on both sides of stitching.

2. On wrong side of rectangle, stitch on broken black line. On right side of rectangle, trim black felt on both sides of stitched lines and from outside and inside of fish. (Do not trim black felt from inside fins.) Trim purple felt from inside sections 1 to 4 to reveal blue plaid fabric. On wrong side of rectangle, stitch on purple lines. On right side of rectangle, trim purple felt from sections 5 to 9 to reveal black felt.

3. Place second rectangle of gold felt on work surface. Place layered rectangle, wrong side up, on felt. Pin at corners. Stitch on brown lines; remove pins. On right side, trim gold felt on both sides of stitched lines. Trim gold from inside star. Place green felt on work surface. Place layered rectangle, wrong side up, in center of felt. Pin at corners. Stitch on green lines; remove pins. On right side of rectangle, trim around green felt.

4. From pink velvet, cut 3½-inch square. Place square, wrong side up, on work surface. Place layered rectangle, wrong side up, on velvet, centering fish head. Pin at corners. Stitch on pink line. On right side of rectangle, trim around velvet. Thread a needle with two strands of embroidery floss; knot end. Bring needle from back to front at fish eye **(refer to template for placement)**. Knot again on right side close to fabric, insert needle at knot, and draw to back. Knot again to secure; trim thread ends.

5. From orange felt, cut 3-inch square. Place layered rectangle wrong side up, on orange square, centering one corner triangle. Pin at corners. Stitch on orange lines; remove pins. On right side, trim around triangle. Repeat with other triangle.

6. Place turquoise felt strip on work surface. Place black felt strip on turquoise. Place layered rectangle, wrong side up, on strips, centering waves on strips. Pin at corners. Stitch on blue line; remove pins. On right side, trim turquoise on both sides of stitched lines. Trim black felt from top edge of waves and from inside waves to reveal purple felt. Place light blue felt strip on work surface. Centering waves on strips, place layered rectangle, wrong side up, on strip. Pin at corners. Stitch on broken blue line. On right side, trim top edge of light blue felt to meet turquoise felt.

7. In center of wrong side of layered rectangle, draw 10½ x 8-inch rectangle for seams. Trim to within ¼ inch of seam lines. From blue print, cut two 2½ x 11-inch strips and two 3¼ x 12½-inch strips. Stitch short strips to top and bottom of rectangle; press. Stitch long strips to rectangle sides; press.

8. From blue print, cut one 16½ x 12-inch rectangle. With right sides together, pin rectangles to pillow top and stitch together, leaving a 6-inch opening along one side; remove pins. Trim excess fabric from corners. Turn right side out. Stuff with fiberfill. Hand-stitch opening closed.

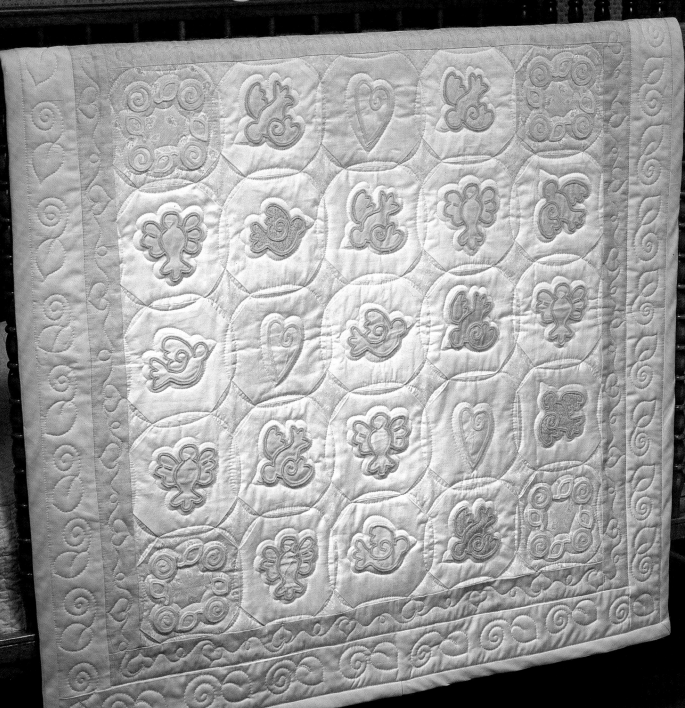

Bird Quilt

On a lovely pastel quilt, endearing birds inhabit a square yard of patchwork sky. Drape this instant heirloom over an antique crib or wrap it around a brand new baby.

Materials

⅓ yard pale pink cotton

⅓ yard pale yellow cotton

⅓ yard cream cotton

⅓ yard mint green print cotton

⅓ yard lime green print cotton

½ yard mint green cotton

⅓ yard blue print cotton

Scraps of pink, pink print, light blue print, light turquoise, turquoise print, and lavender print cotton

¼ yard pink felt

¼ yard blue felt

¼ yard cream felt

⅛ yard yellow felt

39-inch square of cotton for backing

38-inch square of batting

4¼ yards double-fold bias binding

Pink, blue, yellow, and cream thread

Marking pen or pencil

FINISHED SIZE
37 inches square

1. Prepare templates on page 93 (see **Transferring Patterns, page 5**).

2. From pale pink fabric, cut 6-inch square. Draw heart **(Template A, page 93)** in center of wrong side of square. From pink print, cut 4-inch square. From pink felt, cut 4-inch square. Place felt on work surface and place pink print, wrong side up, on felt. Center heart on squares and pin at corners. With pink thread, stitch on marked line; remove pins.

3. On right side of square, trim felt and fabric from around heart. Trim felt from inside heart to reveal pink print. Repeat for total of three squares **(see Photo A)**.

4. From pale yellow fabric, cut 6-inch square. Draw bird **(Template B, page 93)** in center of wrong side of square. From light blue print, cut 4-inch square. From blue felt, cut 4-inch square. Place felt on work surface and place blue print, wrong side up, on felt. Center heart on squares and pin at corners. With blue thread, stitch on marked bird; remove pins. (Do not stitch on beak outline.)

5. On right side of square, trim felt and fabric from around bird. Trim felt from inside bird to reveal blue print. Using **Bird Templates B, C, and D (page 93)**, repeat for total of eighteen squares. Use cream and yellow fabric for backgrounds and pink, pink print, light blue print, light turquoise, turquoise print, and lavender print for bird bodies. All birds are outlined with blue felt.

Photo A

Photo B

Photo C

Photo D

6. From yellow felt, cut 1-inch square. Center beak of one bird on felt square. With yellow thread, stitch on beak outline. On right side of square, trim around beak. Repeat with remaining bird squares **(see Photos B, C, D)**.

7. From mint print, cut 6-inch square. On wrong side of square, center and draw flowers and leaves. From pink print, cut 6-inch square. From pink felt, cut 6-inch square. Place felt on work surface and place pink print, wrong side up, on felt. Center flowers and leaves **(Template E, page 93)** on squares and pin at corners. With pink thread, stitch on marked flowers; remove pins. (Do not stitch on leaves.)

8. On right side of square, trim both felt and fabric from around flowers. Trim felt from inside flowers to reveal pink print. Repeat to make a total of four squares.

9. From cream felt, cut 6-inch square. Center flowers and leaves on felt square and pin at corners. With cream thread, stitch on marked leaves. Remove pins. On right side of square, trim cream felt on both sides of stitched lines. Repeat with remaining flower squares **(see Photo E)**.

Photo E

1³⁄₈"

10. Trim all four corners of each square at a diagonal **(see Diagram A)**. Lay out trimmed squares on work surface, with flowers and leaves in corners, birds and hearts placed randomly. Starting and stopping ¼ inch from each edge, stitch side seams of top five trimmed squares to make one horizontal row. Repeat to make a total of five rows.

11. From lime green print, cut four 2³⁄₈-inch squares **(see Diagram B)**. Starting and stopping ¼ inch from each edge, stitch squares to top row. Repeat with remaining rows. Stitch rows together to make a grid of five trimmed squares across and five down.

12. From blue print, cut four 1³⁄₈-inch squares. With blue squares in corners, stitch remaining squares to recesses around outside edge of grid. Trim corners of squares flush with outside edge of grid; press.

Diagram A

13. From blue print, cut four 2¼ x 29¾-inch strips. Stitch strips to quilt center to make log cabin border **(see Log Cabin Border, page 5)**; press.

14. From mint fabric, cut four 3½ x 34¾-inch strips. Stitch strips to quilt center to make log cabin border; press.

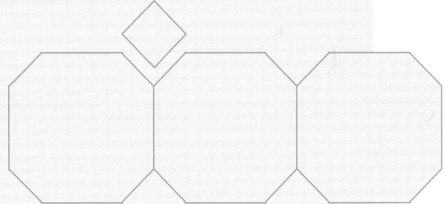

15. With wrong side up, place backing fabric on work surface. Carefully smooth out any folds and center batting on top of backing fabric. With right side up, center quilt top on quilt batting.

Diagram B

16. Pin through all layers or baste with long basting stitches **(see Pinning and Basting, page 5)**. Machine quilt as desired **(see Machine Quilting, page 6)**. Remove pins or basting. Trim edge of quilt. Stitch bias binding around edge of quilt **(see Binding, page 6)**.

Autumn Quilt

Keep chill winds at bay with this sized-just-right border quilt. The autumn motifs of leaves and grapevines move easily into winter. For the pieced borders, choose a variety of colors and prints.

Materials

⅛–¼-yard cuts assorted print fabrics (ten to twelve different prints of same value but different hues)

1 yard brown cotton

¼ yard brown print cotton

¼ yard lavender cotton

1½ yard gray cotton

2 yards burgundy cotton

¾ yard sage green felt

Green thread

52 x 64-inch piece of cotton for backing

51 x 63-inch piece of batting

6¼ yards double-fold bias binding

Marking pen or pencil

FINISHED SIZE
48 x 60 inches

1. Prepare templates on page 94 **(see Transferring Patterns, page 5)**.

2. From assorted prints, cut strips 1 to 3 inches wide and 6 inches long. Stitch together to make one 36½ x 6-inch horizontal row; press. Using the same process but varying the length of the strips accordingly, make one 36½ x 6½-inch row, one 36½ x 4-inch row, and one 36½ x 8-inch row; press.

3. From brown fabric, cut 36½ x 7½-inch rectangle. On wrong side of rectangle, center and draw one leaf. Leaving 1½ inches between each, draw three leaves on each side of center leaf. From brown print, cut 5-inch square. From sage green felt, cut 5-inch square. Place felt on work surface and place brown print, wrong side up, on felt. Center one leaf on square and pin at corners. Stitch on marked line; remove pins.

4. On right side of rectangle, trim both felt and fabric from around leaf. Trim felt from inside leaf to reveal brown print. Repeat with remaining leaves **(see Photo A)**.

5. Using lavender fabric instead of brown print, repeat steps 3 and 4 to make a second leaf row.

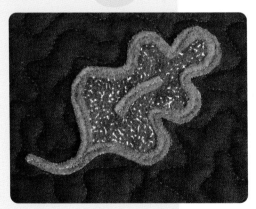

Photo A

6. From brown fabric, cut 36½ x 12-inch rectangle. On wrong side of rectangle, mark center. Leaving ½ inch between each, center and draw four wreaths. From felt, cut 10-inch square. Place felt on work surface and place brown print, wrong side up, on felt. Center one wreath on square and pin at corners. Stitch on marked lines; remove pins.

Photo B

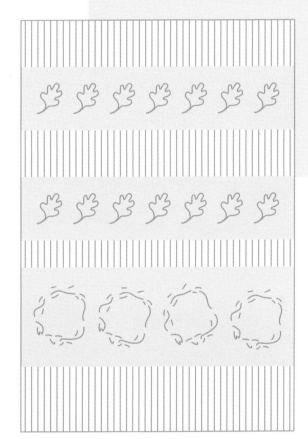

Diagram A

7. On right side of rectangle, trim green felt on both sides of stitched lines. Repeat with remaining wreaths **(see Photo B)**.

8. Stitch rows together **(see Diagram A)**; press.

9. From gray fabric, cut two 2 x 42-inch strips and two 2 x 53-inch strips. Starting and stopping ¼ inch from each edge, center and stitch short strips to top and bottom of quilt center. Starting and stopping ¼ inch from each edge, center and stitch long strips to sides of quilt center. Miter corners **(see Mitered Corners, page 6)**; press.

10. From burgundy fabric, cut two 5½ x 53-inch strips and two 5½ x 65-inch strips. Starting and stopping ¼ inch from each edge, center and stitch short strips to top and bottom of quilt center. Starting and stopping ¼ inch from each edge, center and stitch long strips to sides of quilt center. Miter corners; press.

11. With wrong side up, place backing fabric on work surface. Carefully smooth out any folds and center batting on top of backing fabric. With right side up, center quilt top on quilt batting.

12. Baste through all layers with pins or long basting stitches. Machine quilt as desired **(see Machine Quilting, page 6)**. Remove pins or basting. Trim edge of quilt. Stitch bias binding around edge of quilt **(see Binding, page 6)**.

For a variation on the oak leaf theme, try the Acorn Pillow **(see Photo; template, page 95)**. Layer 12-inch squares of purple felt, black jersey, wine felt, and blue jersey on work surface and follow basic felt layering procedures. Add green felt for the stems, gold felt for the acorns, and gray felt for the acorn tops. Keeping the acorn pieces in place with a small dot of fabric glue, stitch around them with green thread and a wide satin stitch. Use black textured fabric for the background and purple felt for the border.

Acorn Pillow

Botanical Pillows

"Gather ye rosebuds while ye may." The eye-catching border of the Paper Heart Pillow is made from silk flower petals gathered with needle and thread. Along with felt layering, the center square also uses Scherenschnitte, which is explored in "Paper Inspirations" **(see page 60).** The Floating Leaves Pillow features a simple and classic nine-patch layout pairing felt layering with transparent collage **(see page 44).**

Paper Heart Pillow

Materials

⅛ yard dark green cotton

¼ yard cream cotton

⅛ yard white polyester organza

⅛ yard sage green felt

⅓ yard cream print cotton

1¼ yards 1-inch wide green velvet ribbon

⅓ yard green toile fabric

Green and cream thread

10-inch pillow form

Silk flower petals

8 silk leaves, 1⅜ inches long

Air-soluble marking pen

FINISHED SIZE

10 inches square

Photo A

1. Prepare template on page 92 **(see Transferring Patterns, page 5)**.

2. From dark green fabric, cut 4-inch square. Center template on green square, pin in place, and carefully cut out design. For best results it is important to cut accurately, so don't rush this step.

3. From cream fabric, cut 5½-inch square. Center and place heart on cream square. Carefully trim and remove any jagged edges or loose threads.

4. From organza, cut 5½-inch square. Place organza square on cream square. Pin or baste through all layers **(see Pinning and Basting, page 5)**.

5. Adjust sewing machine to straight stitch with about 14 stitches per inch. Using cream thread, carefully stitch around design. Also stitch within flower and within eight border slits. When starting and stopping, reverse direction of stitching for two to three stitches to prevent unraveling. Stitch on cream fabric as closely as possible to green fabric. The machine stitches will hold threads of cut edge in place. Do not stitch on green fabric. **(See introduction to "Paper Inspirations," page 61.)** Remove pins or basting.

6. With marking pen, draw 3¾-inch square, centered on back of heart square. From felt, cut 4½-inch square. Place felt on work surface. Place stitched square, wrong side up, on felt. Center marked square on felt square and pin in place at corners. With green thread, stitch on marked line; remove pins. On right side of square, trim around square. Also carefully trim felt from inside square to reveal heart.

7. From cream print, cut four 3 x 8-inch strips. Stitch strips to square to make log cabin border **(see Log Cabin Border, page 5)**; press.

8. With cream thread, hand-stitch silk flower petals **(see Photo A)** to seam line **(see Diagram A)**. Come up from back, thread several petals on needle, gather petals, and stitch through fabric at seam to secure. Continue this process to complete flower border.

9. From toile fabric, cut 10½-inch square. With wrong sides together, pin square to pillow top. Stitch together leaving 7-inch opening along one side; remove pins. Insert pillow form. Hand-stitch opening closed.

10. Hand-stitch one edge of ribbon to stitching line of exposed seam. Wrap ribbon around seam to cover exposed edge and hand-stitch opposite ribbon edge to stitching line on back of pillow. Fold at corners. Where ends meet, overlap slightly, turn top end under, and stitch to opposite end.

11. Hand-stitch two leaves in place at each corner **(see Photo B)**.

12. Roll in each corner and hand-stitch in place.

Diagram A

Photo B

Floating Leaves Pillow

Materials

½ yard white cotton

½ yard gray polyester organza

¼ yard sage green felt

9 silk leaves, 1⅜ inches long

Green thread

12-inch pillow form

Air-soluble marking pen

Fabric glue

FINISHED SIZE

12 inches square

1. From white fabric, cut 12½-inch square. With marking pen, draw 7½-inch square, centered on back of white square. Divide drawn square at 2½ and 5 inches in both directions to create a grid of nine squares. Place small dot of glue on wrong side of each leaf. On right side of fabric, place a leaf diagonally in center of each square.

2. From organza, cut 12½-inch square. Layer organza on square. Stitch a line down center of each leaf through all layers, extending ½ inch at bottom to form stem. When starting and stopping, reverse direction of stitching for two to three stitches to prevent unraveling.

3. From felt, cut 9-inch square. Place felt on work surface. Place pillow top, wrong side up, on felt. Center marked square and pin at corners. Stitch on marked lines. On right side of square, trim around square. Also trim felt from inside squares to reveal leaves.

4. From white fabric, cut second 12½-inch square. With right sides together, pin square to pillow top. Stitch together, leaving 7-inch opening along one side. Remove pins. Trim excess fabric at corners. Turn right side out. Insert pillow form. Hand-stitch opening closed.

Yarn Painting

Yarn painting is loosely based on the modern folk art of the Huichol Indians of northern Mexico, whose fluid and complex compositions represent the relationship between humans, nature, and the gods. Their process involves spreading melted beeswax on a solid substrate such as a board; the wax is etched with a design into which strands of yarn are embedded until the entire surface is covered. Like the traditional version, this approach covers the entire working surface, but here the yarn is first applied to cloth with glue, then a stitched grid permanently holds the individual ends and loops in place. These simplified designs can be integrated into quilts, pillows, and other soft items.

All projects are worked with inexpensive four-ply acrylic yarn, available in many colors and plush enough to cover well. Mark designs with black colored pencil (glue makes water-soluble marker run; number 2 pencil is not dark enough). Cotton fabric is the best backing since it takes glue well and dries evenly. Work on a slightly padded surface such as an ironing board so you can pin the yarn ends in place during drying. (First cover the surface with plastic wrap to protect it from glue seepage.) You'll also need water-soluble stabilizer to stitch the grid.

Basic Instructions

1. Draw design on backing fabric.

2. Apply thin layer of fabric glue to small area of fabric **(see Photos A, B)**. Place yarn snugly against itself, coiling or swirling onto fabric, or apply in individual strands **(see diagrams)**. If glue dries before yarn is applied, add second thin layer. Let project sit overnight so it's completely dry before stitching.

3. Lay stabilizer over design area and stitch diagonal grid pattern over yarn, spacing lines about ⅜ inch apart **(see Photo C)**.

4. Following manufacturer's directions, immerse piece in water to dissolve stabilizer **(see Photo D)**. Immerse project just long enough to dissolve stabilizer. If left in water too long, glue will also dissolve.

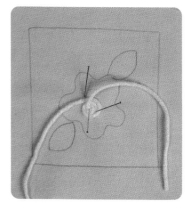
Photo A

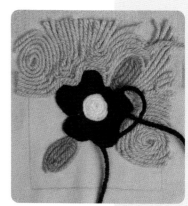
Photo B

Helpful Hints

✻ The hardest part of this technique is securing cut ends. When ending a section, pin yarn in place and cut ends 1–1½ inches past pin. After 5–10 minutes drying, remove pins and trim ends.

✻ Have lots of pins. Glue will dry on them, making them unsuitable for regular sewing projects, so discard them or save for future yarn painting.

✻ Stitch grid with sewing thread to add a subtle design element. To make grid disappear, stitch with nylon thread.

✻ When assembling finished project, keep iron temperature low and press *only* the seams. Do not place iron directly on yarn because acrylic fibers will melt.

✻ Yarn manipulation takes some practice, so start with a small project, such as a square from the **Thank-a-Sheep Quilt (see pages 36–39)**. If you decide not to complete the whole quilt, glue the trimmed square to a blank greeting card.

  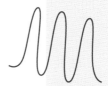

Applying yarn in various patterns

Photo C

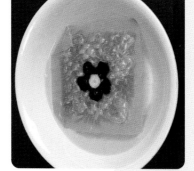
Photo D

29

Skeleton Key Pillow

In days gone by, skeleton keys were forged from iron. This key is shaped from black yarn and adorned with a fanciful border. Unlock your memories of Great-grandmother's unwieldy key ring with this graphic accent pillow.

Materials

9¼ x 7 inches light blue fabric for backing

⅛ yard wine cotton fabric

Scrap of red print fabric

½ yard white floral-print cotton

Four-ply acrylic yarn in black, lavender, wine, and light blue

9¼ x 7 inches water-soluble stabilizer

Polyester fiberfill

Nylon thread

Maroon thread

Black colored pencil

Water-soluble marking pen

Straightedge

Fabric glue

FINISHED SIZE

14 x 11½ inches

1. Prepare templates on pages 97 and 98 **(see Transferring Patterns, page 5)**. With black pencil, draw design on backing fabric. Glue yarn to backing following basic instructions on page 29, starting with key and working out to edges, pinning as necessary. Let glue dry overnight.

2. With marking pen and straightedge, draw diagonal grid on stabilizer. Place stabilizer on yarn design and pin in place at corners. Stitch on marked lines with nylon thread.

3. Following manufacturer's directions, immerse piece in water to dissolve stabilizer. Let dry.

4. For seam lines, draw 8¼ x 6-inch rectangle, centered on wrong side of piece. Trim to within ¼ inch of marked lines.

5. From wine fabric, cut two 1⅛ x 8¾-inch strips and two 1⅛ x 6½-inch strips. With maroon thread, stitch longer strips to top and bottom of yarn rectangle and shorter strips to sides. Press fabric seams only. (Do not place hot iron on acrylic yarn.)

6. From red print, cut four triangles **(see template, page 98)** and stitch to corners of rectangle. Trim excess wine fabric from behind triangles; press seams.

7. From floral print, cut two 10 x 2¾-inch strips and two 12¼ x 2¾ -inch strips. Stitch shorter strips to top and bottom of rectangle; press. Stitch longer strips to sides of rectangle; press.

8. From white floral fabric, cut a 14½ x 12¼-inch rectangle. Pin it to pillow top, right sides together. Stitch, leaving 5-inch opening along one side. Remove pins. Trim excess fabric from corners. Turn right side out, stuff with fiberfill, and hand-stitch opening closed.

Cherries Jubilee
Neck Roll

O

ne bunch of cherries is turned and twisted to make this charming pillow, a delicious example of botanical eye candy.

Materials

6 x 16¾-inch rectangle cream fabric for backing

⅛ yard mauve checked fabric

¼ yard rust textured fabric

Four-ply acrylic yarn in purple, green, wine, and cream

6 x 16¾-inch rectangle water-soluble stabilizer

10-inch neck roll pillow form

Nylon thread

Rust thread

Black colored pencil

Water-soluble marking pen

Fabric glue

FINISHED SIZE

11 x 5 x 5 inches

1. Prepare template on page 98 (see **Transferring Patterns, page 5**). With black pencil, draw design on backing. Starting with a cherry, glue yarn to backing following basic instructions on page 29. Working from center out, complete design (see **Photo A**). Let glue dry overnight.

2. With marking pen, draw straight grid on stabilizer. Place stabilizer on yarn design and pin in place at corners. With nylon thread, stitch on marked lines.

3. Following manufacturer's directions, immerse piece in water to dissolve stabilizer. Let dry.

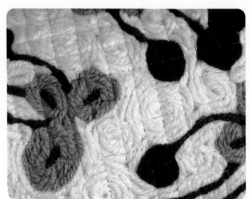

Photo A

4. For seam lines, draw 5 x 15¾-inch rectangle, centered on wrong side of piece. Trim to within ¼ inch of marked lines.

5. From checked fabric, cut two 1¼ x 16¼-inch strips. With regular thread, stitch strips to long sides of yarn rectangle; press. (*Note:* Press fabric seams only. Do not place iron on acrylic yarn.)

6. From rust fabric, cut two 5½ x 16¼-inch strips. Stitch strips to sides of rectangle; press.

7. With right sides together, fold rectangle in half lengthwise. Stitch short sides together to form tube. Turn right side out. Insert pillow form in center of tube. Fold one side of fabric to make flange extending ½ inch past pillow form. Hand-stitch at pillow edge. Repeat on opposite side. Turn fabric edge under ½ inch and hand-stitch running stitch along folded edge. Gather thread tightly and knot to close end. Repeat on opposite side (see **Photo B**).

Photo B

Bird and Berries Pillow

A true mixed-media project, this charming pillow combines yarn painting and collage techniques, with fabric painting and embroidery thrown in for good measure.

Materials

8 inches cream fabric for backing

⅓ yard black felt

Scraps of red and purple felt

¼ yard white silk organza

Four-ply acrylic yarn in sea foam green, dark blue, and red

8-inch square water-soluble stabilizer

Polyester fiberfill

Green thread

Black, mint, and cream embroidery floss

Black colored pencil

Air-soluble marking pen

Water-soluble marking pen

White acrylic paint

Stencil brush

5 paper feathers, assorted sizes, 1¾–2¾ inches long

Fabric glue

FINISHED SIZE

10½ inches square

1. Prepare template on page 92 **(see Transferring Patterns, page 5)**. With black pencil, draw design on backing fabric. Starting in center, glue yarn to backing fabric following basic instructions on page 29. Working from center out, complete design. Let glue dry overnight.

2. With water-soluble marking pen, draw diagonal grid on stabilizer. Place stabilizer on yarn design and pin in place at corners. With green thread, stitch on marked lines.

3. Following manufacturer's directions, immerse piece in water to dissolve stabilizer. Let dry.

4. For seam lines, draw 7-inch square, centered on wrong side of piece. Trim to within ¼ inch of marked lines.

5. Place tracing of bird template on purple felt, trace around shape with air-soluble marking pen, and cut along marked line. Apply small amount of white paint to stencil brush; blot on paper towel. Holding brush perpendicular to work surface, apply thin layer of paint to bird in light pouncing motion. Let dry.

6. From black felt, cut 3¼-inch circle. Center bird on circle. Embroider details on bird **(see Diagram A for colors and placement)**. (For details on stitches, consult a basic embroidery guide or check the Internet.) Center black circle on yarn square and hand-stitch in place.

7. From red felt, cut seven circles, each ⅝ inch in diameter. Place randomly around large circle and hand-stitch in place. With black floss, add stems to selected berries using stem stitch. Dip pencil or wrong end of paintbrush in white paint. Dot selected berries with paint to add highlights. Let dry.

8. From black felt, cut four 2¼ x 9¼-inch strips. Place small dot of glue on wrong side of each paper feather. Place them on felt strips within ¼ inch of edges. From organza, cut four 2¼ x 9¼-inch strips. Layer organza strips on felt strips. Stitch strips to square to make log cabin border **(see Log Cabin Border, page 5)**; press. (*Note:* Press felt seams only. Do not place hot iron on acrylic yarn.)

9. From black felt, cut 11-inch square. With right sides together, pin felt square to yarn square. Stitch together leaving 5-inch opening along one side; remove pins. Trim excess felt at corners. Turn right side out. Stuff with fiberfill. Hand-stitch opening closed.

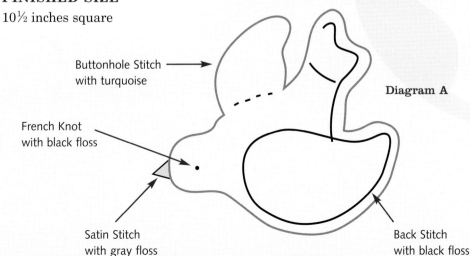

Diagram A

Buttonhole Stitch with turquoise

French Knot with black floss

Satin Stitch with gray floss

Back Stitch with black floss

Bird and Berries Pillow 35

Thank-a-Sheep Quilt

Materials

¼ yard green cotton for sweater blocks

¼ yard blue cotton for stocking blocks

¼ yard tan print fabric for mitten blocks

¼ yard lavender cotton for sheep blocks

⅛ yard green cotton for sweater block borders

⅛ yard blue print cotton for stocking block borders

⅛ yard lavender print cotton for mitten block borders

⅛ yard cream flannel

½ yard cream cotton

⅓ yard light turquoise cotton

½ yard blue toile fabric

Four-ply acrylic yarn in cream, lavender, medium blue, dark blue, and green

Curly cream yarn

38-inch square of cotton for quilt backing

37-inch square of batting

Nylon thread

Cream thread

Black colored pencil

Air-soluble marking pen

Fabric glue

FINISHED SIZE

36 inches square

ave you hugged a lamb today? If fuzzy sweaters, stockings, and mittens keep you warm, take time to thank a sheep. Hanging this small quilt on the wall or draping it over a chair is the perfect way to warm up a space. Since the yarn-covered squares are small, there's no need to secure them with a stitched grid. Instead, random lines are stitched over the yarn surface, eliminating the need for stabilizer and all the steps it entails.

1. From green fabric, cut five 5 x 4-inch rectangles. Prepare templates on pages 99–100 **(see Transferring Patterns, page 5)**. With black pencil, draw sweater centered in each rectangle. Starting in center of one rectangle, glue yarn to backing fabric following basic instructions on page 29. Complete design. Repeat for remaining rectangles. Let glue dry overnight **(see Photo A)**.

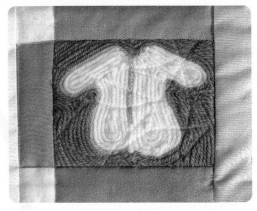

Photo A

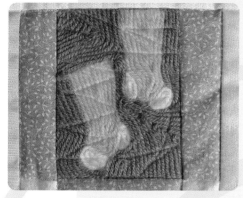

Photo B

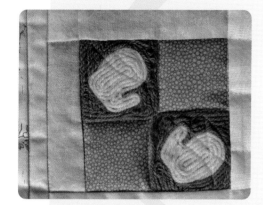

Photo C

Photo D

2. From blue fabric, cut four 4 x 5-inch rectangles. With black pencil, draw a pair of stockings, centered in each rectangle. Refer to step 1 to complete squares (see Photo B).

3. From tan print, cut five 5-inch squares. With marking pen, draw lines to divide square into quarters. With black pencil, draw mittens in top right and bottom left quadrants. Refer to step 1 to complete squares (see Photo C).

4. From lavender fabric, cut four 6 x 6-inch squares. With black pencil, draw a sheep, centered on each square. Fill in face, ears, legs, and background areas of one square. Lightly coat sheep body with fabric glue and loosely pile curly yarn on exposed glue. Pin in place. Repeat for remaining squares (see Photo D).

5. With nylon thread, stitch random lines on yarn designs to secure. For sheep squares, stitch on background area only.

6. On wrong sides of yarn squares, draw seam lines as follows, centered in squares: sweaters, 4 x 3 inches; stockings, 3 x 4 inches; mittens, 4 x 4 inches; sheep, 5 x 5 inches. Trim to within ¼ inch of marked lines.

7. Thread machine and bobbin with cream thread.

8. From medium green fabric, cut two 4½ x 1½-inch and one 1½ x 3½-inch strips. From flannel, cut two 1½-inch squares. Stitch strips and squares to one sweater rectangle (see Diagram A). Repeat for remaining sweater rectangles.

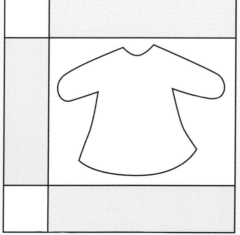

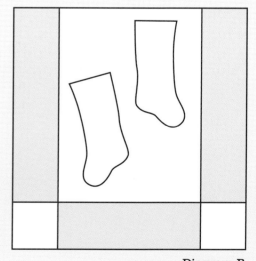

Diagram A

Diagram B

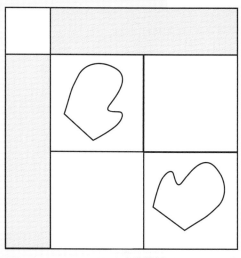

Diagram C

9. From blue print, cut two 1½ x 4½-inch and one 3½ x 1½-inch strips. From flannel, cut two 1½-inch squares. Stitch strips and squares to one stocking rectangle **(see Diagram B)**. Repeat for remaining stocking rectangles.

10. From lavender print, cut two 1 x 4½-inch strips. From flannel, cut 1½-inch square. Stitch strips and square to mitten square **(see Diagram C)**. Repeat for remaining mitten squares.

11. From cream fabric, cut two 5½-inch squares. Make one sweater/mittens square **(see Diagram D)**; press. (*Note:* Press fabric seams only. Do not place hot iron on acrylic yarn.) Seams will be bulky where yarn squares intersect. Clip seam allowances at corners **(see Diagram E)**. Repeat to make a total of five squares.

12. From light turquoise fabric, cut two 5½-inch squares. Make one stocking/sheep square **(see Diagram F)**; press. Repeat for total of four squares.

13. Alternating combined squares, stitch squares together to make a grid of three across and three down; press.

14. From cream fabric, cut four 1¼ x 32-inch strips. Center and stitch strips to sides of quilt top, starting and stopping ¼ inch from each edge. Miter corners **(see Mitered Corners, page 6)**; press.

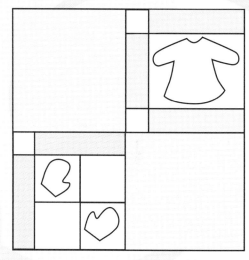

Diagram D

15. From toile fabric, cut four 3¼ x 37-inch strips. Center and stitch strips to sides of quilt top, starting and stopping ¼ inch from each edge. Miter corners; press.

16. With wrong side up, place quilt backing fabric on work surface. Carefully smooth out folds and center batting on top of backing fabric. With right side up, center quilt top on quilt batting.

17. Pin through all layers or baste with long basting stitches **(see Pinning and Basting, page 5)**. Machine quilt as desired **(see Machine Quilting, page 6)**. Remove pins or basting. Trim thread ends. Trim edge of quilt. Stitch facing to quilt **(see Facing, page 7)**.

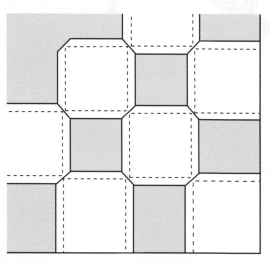

Diagram E

Diagram F

Gently Down the Stream Quilt

The yarn square in the center of this medallion quilt is reminiscent of paint-by-number kits popular during the fifties and sixties. The primitive shading and the streaks of highlights give this ship a nostalgic timber ideal for gracing your family room or den.

Materials

9-inch square light blue fabric for backing

¼ yard wine cotton

½ yard green-and-blue striped cotton fabric

Scrap of teal print cotton

⅛ yard red print cotton

⅛ yard olive print cotton

¼ yard blue print cotton

¼ yard green metallic fabric

Scrap of olive fabric cotton

Four-ply acrylic yarn in black, lavender, wine, medium blue, dark blue, white, cream, yellow, light gray, and light green

9-inch square water-soluble stabilizer

30-inch square of cotton for backing

29-inch square of batting

Nylon thread

Tan thread

Black colored pencil

Water-soluble marking pen

Fabric glue

FINISHED SIZE

28 inches square

1. Prepare template on page 43 (see **Transferring Patterns, page 5**). With black pencil, draw design on light blue fabric. Starting with large sail, glue yarn to fabric following basic instructions on page 29. Working from center out, complete design. Let glue dry overnight

2. With marking pen, draw diagonal grid on stabilizer. Place stabilizer on yarn design and pin in place at corners. With nylon thread, stitch on marked line. **(see Photo A).**

3. Following manufacturer's directions, immerse piece in water to dissolve stabilizer. Let dry.

4. For seam lines, draw 7¾-inch square, centered on wrong side of yarn square. Trim to within ¼ inch of marked lines.

Photo A

Photo B

5. From wine fabric, cut four 1¾ x 10 ¾-inch strips. Center strips around sides of yarn square and stitch with tan thread, starting and stopping ¼ inch from each edge; press. (*Note:* Press fabric seams only. Do not place hot iron on acrylic yarn.) Miter corners **(see Mitered Corners, page 6)**.

6. From striped fabric, cut four 2⅞ x 15½-inch strips. Stitch two of the strips to top and bottom of design square; press. From teal print, cut four 2⅞-inch squares. Stitch squares to ends of remaining strips. Stitch strips to sides of design square; press.

7. From red print, cut four 1⅛ x 5½-inch strips. From olive fabric, cut four 1⅛-inch squares. Referring to step 7, stitch strips and squares to design square.

8. From blue print, cut four 1½ x 18¾-inch strips. Center strips around sides of design square, starting and stopping ¼ inch from each edge. Miter corners; press.

9. From metallic fabric, cut two 18¾ x 2-inch strips. Stitch strips to top and bottom of design square; press. Cut two 2½ x 22¾-inch strips. Stitch strips to sides of design square; press.

10. From striped fabric, cut four 4 x 29-inch strips. From olive print, cut four 4¼-inch squares. Referring to step 7, stitch strips and squares to design square **(see Photo B)**.

11. Hand-stitch "rigging" yarns to ship. Knot and trim yarn ends.

12. With wrong side up, place backing fabric on work surface. Carefully smooth out folds and center batting on top of backing fabric. With right side up, center quilt top on quilt batting.

13. Pin through all layers or baste with long basting stitches **(see Pinning and Basting, page 5)**. Machine quilt as desired **(see Machine Quilting, page 6)**. Remove pins or basting. Trim thread ends. Trim edge of quilt. Stitch facing to quilt **(see Facing, page 7)**.

Template A (please copy at 110%).

Transparent Collage

When is confetti a work of art? When it is incorporated into a unique fabric collage. A collage is a collection of sometimes coordinating and sometimes disparate objects united in a composition. The artistry lies in selecting the right combination of materials and placing them in an aesthetic arrangement. Often sentimental objects are stirred into the mix—those that evoke a memory or a sense of place.

They can be simple or complex, but the best collages are infused with life and can spirit us away to a place that is familiar or simply imaginary. This art form is the perfect expression for collectors because they can see the beauty and potential in the common: bits of ribbon, dried leaves, canceled postage stamps, and other found objects.

The elements of a paper collage are arranged within the boundaries of the paper's edge. If objects are three-dimensional or if the surface is built up to become three-dimensional, it is called relief collage. Paper collage has experienced a surge in interest recently with the advent of scrapbooking. Scrapbook enthusiasts may not consider themselves collage artists, but scrapbooking consists of arranging a collection of objects on a sheet of paper and certainly fits within the definition of collage.

The word *collage* is French for "to paste," but since pasting in this case is replaced by stitching, perhaps we should call this "sewllage." The projects in this chapter are made from fabric instead of paper, and are arranged within the border of a quilt, the edges of a throw pillow, and the inside of a display frame. Fabric collage can consist of a composition of fabric only, or it can include nonfiber accents.

These projects utilize transparent fabrics because transparency adds interest to the layering aspect of collage. Who can resist picking up a snow globe or looking through a keyhole just to see what is inside? Now, instead of asking what is inside, the question becomes, What is underneath? Sophisticated projects are achieved by overlaying a design with another design, resulting in lovely, lustrous depth.

Basic Instructions

The basic steps for assembly will vary from project to project, so specific how-to instructions and in-progress photos are presented with the individual projects rather than in the chapter introduction.

Helpful Hints

❋ Since fabric collage requires more handling than paper collage, the accent pieces must be sturdier than those used for paper collage. Paper objects usually don't work unless they are small.

❋ Straight pins are used during assembly, and machine stitching secures the objects and the layers to the background.

Sun and Butterfly Framed Collage

Coloring stamped images with colored pencils rather than fabric markers yields softer edges and subtler colors. After completing this layered project, experiment with other types of sheer fabrics such as voile and chiffon.

Materials

⅓ yard white cotton

⅓ yard violet cotton

6 x 7-inch pieces of dark blue, turquoise, and yellow polyester organza

1 yard silver grosgrain ribbon, ⅛ inch wide

Turquoise thread

Sun stamp, about 1⅞ inches in diameter

Butterfly stamp, about 1⅝ x ¾ inches

Brown ink pad

Colored pencils

Fiberfill for stuffing

Water-soluble marking pen

Premade frame, 10 x 12 inches

Picture mat to fit frame, with 6 x 6¾-inch window

FINISHED SIZE
11½ x 12½ inches

1. Prepare template on page 101 (**see Transferring Patterns, page 5**).

2. From white fabric, cut 11 x 13-inch rectangle. From violet fabric, cut 11 x 13-inch rectangle. With marking pen, trace border on dark blue organza. Layer fabric on work surface in this order: white fabric, violet fabric, turquoise organza, and dark blue organza, centering the small rectangles on the large ones. Pin or baste through all layers (**see Pinning and Basting, page 5**). Stitch on marked lines.

3. Trim dark blue organza and turquoise organza from around notched border to reveal violet fabric. Trim dark blue organza, turquoise organza, and violet fabric from inside narrow border to reveal white fabric. Trim dark blue organza from between notched border and narrow border to reveal turquoise organza.

4. Using brown ink pad, stamp sun near top of white rectangle. Stamp butterfly below sun (see photo of finished project for placement). Let dry. Color in sun and butterfly with colored pencils.

5. From white fabric, cut 6 x 7-inch rectangle. Place on work surface. Center stitched design, right side up, on white fabric. Center yellow organza on stitched design. Pin at corners. Stitch along inside and outside of narrow border. Stitch around butterfly. Adjust sewing machine to narrow satin stitch and stitch around sun. Trim yellow organza to reveal sun, and around narrow border to reveal turquoise organza. On wrong side of stitched design, trim white fabric from around stitched lines.

6. From ribbon, cut four 5½-inch lengths. Center ribbon pieces along narrow blue border. Adjust machine to narrow zigzag stitch with about 14 stitches per inch. Stitch on ribbon, changing direction at corners. Trim ribbon ends.

7. On wrong side of stitched design, cut small diagonal slit in circle through backing layer only. Stuff small amount of fiberfill in circle to pad sun design (**see Photo A**). Hand-stitch slit closed.

Photo A

8. Insert rectangle into mat and frame. If you prefer, have the piece professionally stretched and framed.

Light-as-Air Pillows

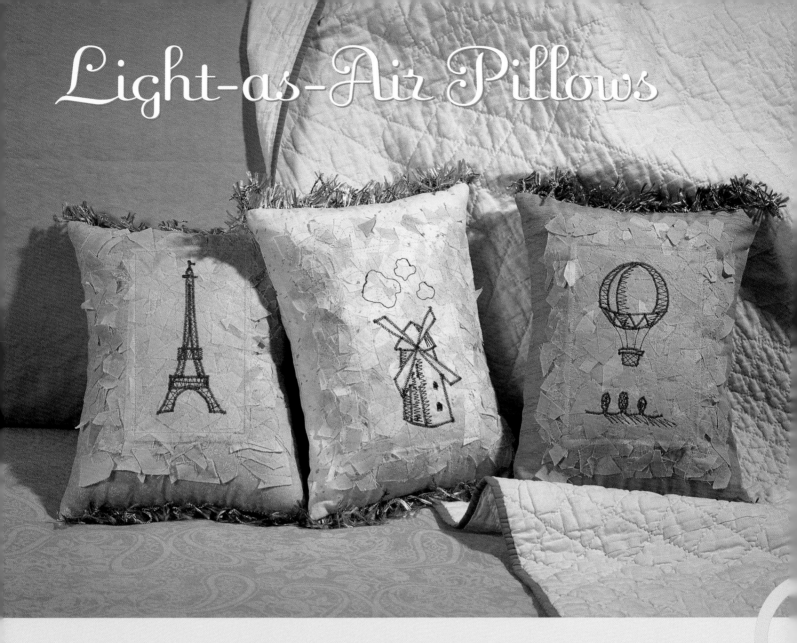

S himmery translucent layers add depth to a trio of pillows whose delicate designs seem to float over the surface. The layering lends implied space or "air" between the layers.

Eiffel Tower Pillow

The outline of a beloved icon sits on a layer of filmy white fabric with a melange of carefully arranged pastels beneath.

Materials

⅓ yard light blue print cotton

Scraps of light blue, light blue print, medium blue, lavender, and pink cotton

White polyester organza

½ yard gray-green fringe trim

Light blue and gray thread

Water-soluble stabilizer

Air-soluble marking pen

Polyester fiberfill

FINISHED SIZE:
8 x 10 inches

Photo A

1. From light blue print, cut 9 x 11-inch rectangle. With marking pen, draw 6½ x 8½-inch rectangle, centered on fabric. From fabric scraps, cut irregular snippets measuring ½ to 1½ inches. Arrange snippets within marked area, overlapping them slightly **(see Photo A)**.

2. Place 9 x 11-inch piece of stabilizer over arranged snippets and pin in place in random areas about 2 inches apart. Handle carefully so as not to move unpinned snippets.

3. Using light blue thread, machine-stitch a random curvilinear pattern over area, making sure to stitch through each snippet at least once.

4. Following manufacturer's directions, immerse piece in water to dissolve stabilizer. Let dry; press. Trim to 8½ x 10½ inches.

5. Cut 4½ x 7¼-inch piece of organza. With marking pen, draw design, centered on organza **(see template, page 100)**. Center organza over stitched snippets and pin. Adjust sewing machine to narrow zigzag with about 40 stitches per inch. Using gray thread, carefully stitch on marked design through all layers. Fill in with wide zigzag stitches and straight stitches **(see Photo B)**.

6. Trim threads. With marking pen, draw 3¼ x 6-inch rectangle, centered around tower. Using light blue thread, stitch along marked line. Trim threads. Trim organza to within ¼ inch of stitching line.

7. Cut two 9-inch lengths of fringe. Pin or baste bound edge of one length of fringe to one short end of pillow, with fringe pointing toward center of pillow top **(see Diagram A, page 50)**. Repeat with second length on opposite side of pillow top. From light blue print, cut 8½ x 10½-inch rectangle. Pin rectangle to pillow top, right sides together. Stitch, leaving 4-inch opening along one side. Trim excess fabric from corners. Turn right side out, press, stuff firmly with fiberfill, and hand-stitch opening closed.

Photo B

Windmill Pillow

Try this delightfully pastoral windmill pillow as an accent for a diminutive chair.

Materials

⅓ yard cream print cotton

Scraps of light blue, lavender, cream, and tan cotton

White polyester organza

½ yard taupe fringe

White and brown thread

Water-soluble stabilizer

Air-soluble marking pen

Polyester fiberfill

FINISHED SIZE

8 x 10 inches

1. From cream print, cut 9 x 11-inch rectangle. Draw 6½ x 8½-inch rectangle, centered on fabric. From fabric scraps, cut irregular snippets measuring ½ to 1½ inches. Arrange snippets within marked area, overlapping them slightly **(see step 1 of Eiffel Tower Pillow, page 49)**.

2. Complete steps 2 through 4 of **Eiffel Tower Pillow**, stitching with white thread.

3. Cut 4¾ x 7¼-inch piece of organza. With marking pen, draw design, centered on organza **(see template, page 101)**. Center organza over stitched snippets and pin. Adjust sewing machine to narrow zigzag with about 40 stitches per inch. Using brown thread, carefully stitch building and blades through all layers. Fill in with straight stitches **(see Photo A)**. Trim thread ends. With marking pen, draw 3½ x 6-inch rectangle, centered around design. Using white thread, stitch along marked line. Trim thread ends. Trim organza to within ¼ inch of stitching line.

4. Complete step 7 of **Eiffel Tower Pillow** **(see Diagram A)**, using cream print for backing and taupe fringe.

Diagram A

Photo A

Hot-Air Balloon Pillow

Let this turn-of-the-century balloon hover atop bed pillows or float across a lofty throw.

Materials

⅓ yard light gray print cotton

Scraps of light blue, light green, lavender, turquoise, and cream cotton

White polyester organza

½ yard gray/blue fringe

White and green thread

Water-soluble stabilizer

Air-soluble marking pen

Polyester fiberfill

FINISHED SIZE
8 x 10 inches

1. From light gray print, cut 9 x 11-inch rectangle. Draw 6½ x 8½-inch rectangle, centered on fabric. From fabric scraps, cut irregular snippets measuring ½ to 1½ inches. Arrange snippets within marked area, overlapping them slightly **(see step 1 of Eiffel Tower Pillow, page 49).**

2. Complete steps 2 through 4 of Eiffel Tower Pillow, stitching with white thread.

3. Cut 5 x 7-inch piece of organza. With marking pen, draw design, centered on organza **(see template, page 101).** Center organza over stitched snippets and pin. Adjust sewing machine to narrow satin stitch. Using green thread, carefully stitch outlines of balloon, basket, and trees through all layers. Fill in with straight stitches **(see Photo A).** Trim thread ends. With marking pen, draw 3¾ x 5¾-inch rectangle, centered around design. Using white thread, stitch along marked line. Trim thread ends. Trim organza to within ¼ inch of stitching line.

4. Complete step 7 of **Eiffel Tower Pillow**, using gray print for backing and gray/blue fringe.

Photo A

Framed Asian Montage

Layering different colors of organza on white fabric is like mixing watercolor paint on white paper. The colors change while the white background shows through, keeping the tone bright.

Materials

½ yard white cotton

Scrap of Asian print cotton

Scraps of dark blue, light blue, and taupe polyester organza

¼ yard turquoise organza

¼ yard cream organza

⅓ yard yellow print cotton

¼ yard gold grosgrain ribbon, ⅛ inch wide

Tan thread

Bird stamp, about 1⅞ x 2⅛ inches

Cherry stamp, about 1¼ x 1½ inches

Brown ink pad

Two silk oak leaves, about 1½ x 2 inches

Key charm

Air-soluble marking pen

Fabric glue

Premade frame, 12 x 14 inches

Picture mat to fit frame, with 7½ x 9⅜-inch window

FINISHED SIZE

13 x 15 inches

1. From white fabric, cut 13 x 15-inch rectangle. Draw rectangle and dividing lines, centered on white fabric **(see Diagram A)**. With brown ink, stamp bird at top left and two cherry images at bottom right. Let dry.

2. Prepare templates on pages 94–95 **(see Transferring Patterns, page 5)**. Pin kimono to Asian print, trace around shape with marking pen; cut along marked line. Place small dot of glue in center of wrong side of kimono and adhere in large area of white background. From dark blue organza, cut 2 x 2-inch square. Place small dot of glue in center of square and adhere in middle bottom section. Trim one leaf to make it slightly smaller than its mate. Place small dot of glue on wrong side of each leaf. Adhere small leaf next to kimono and large leaf on dark blue square.

3. From light and dark blue organza, cut irregular-size confetti for top right and bottom left corners. Arrange confetti in designated sections.

4. From turquoise organza, cut 9 x 11-inch rectangle. Place organza over design area. From cream organza cut 9 x 11-inch rectangle. Place cream organza over turquoise organza. Pin through all layers at corners. Stitch on marked lines and around kimono. Trim cream organza from top left and bottom right section to reveal turquoise organza.

5. From taupe organza, cut 3¼ x 6½-inch rectangle and 4¾ x 2½-inch rectangle. Draw overlay designs, centered on each rectangle. Center each rectangle on design, pin, and stitch where indicated. Carefully trim around overlays to within ⅛ inch of stitching lines.

6. With marking pen, draw 6⅜ x 8¼-inch rectangle for stitching lines, centered on wrong side of white fabric. Trim to within ¼ inch of marked lines. From yellow print, cut two 11 x 3-inch strips. Center strips along top and bottom edges of rectangle and stitch, starting and stopping ¼ inch from each edge. Cut two 3 x 14-inch strips. Center strips along sides of rectangle and stitch, starting and stopping ¼ inch from each edge. Miter corners **(see Mitered Corners, page 6)**.

7. From ribbon, cut three 2½-inch lengths. Place two along kimono border. Adjust machine to narrow zigzag with about 14 stitches per inch. Stitch on ribbon. When starting and stopping, reverse direction for two or three stitches to prevent unraveling. Trim thread ends. Thread charm onto remaining ribbon. Fold ribbon in half and hand stitch to kimono collar.

8. Insert rectangle into mat and frame. If you prefer, have the piece professionally stretched and framed.

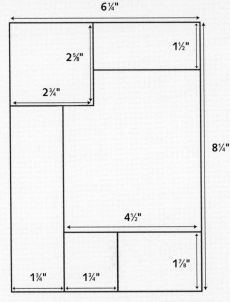

6¼"

1½"

2⅝"

2¾"

8¼"

4½"

1⅞"

1¾"   1¾"

Diagram A

Kimono Quilt

Dried flower sachets are made with open-weave fabric so the fragrance can be released. These kimonos resemble fragile sachets but the focus is on the beauty of the flowers rather than on their scent. Use sturdy flowers such as angel wings or delphinium. For the green organza, choose very sheer polyester with just a slight tint of green.

Materials

¼ yard purple cotton

¼ yard burgundy cotton

½ yard dark brown cotton

¼ yard medium brown cotton

½ yard tan fabric

¼ yard striped gold silk fabric

¼ yard gold silk fabric

6 x 7-inch piece gold moiré fabric

¼ yard lavender cotton

¼ yard green polyester organza

Scrap of cream cotton

¾ yard white silk organza

Red pressed flower petals

Blue pressed flower petals

Tan, lavender, and cream thread

32 x 42-inch piece of batting

33 x 43-inch piece of cotton for backing

Marking pen or pencil

FINISHED SIZE
31 x 41 inches

1. From purple fabric, cut six 6 x 6¾-inch rectangles. From burgundy fabric, cut six 6 x 6¾-inch rectangles. From dark brown fabric, cut eight 6 x 6¾-inch rectangles.

2. From medium brown fabric, cut three 1⅜ x 6-inch strips. Stitch strips between rectangles to make top horizontal row (**see Diagram A for sequence**). Repeat for second, third, fourth, and bottom rows; press.

3. From medium brown fabric, cut six 25⅛ x 1⅜-inch strips. Stitch four strips between horizontal rows. Stitch remaining strips to top and bottom of pieced section; press. Cut two 1⅜ x 37-inch strips. Stitch strips to sides of pieced section; press.

4. From tan fabric, cut two 3 x 37-inch strips. Stitch strips to sides of pieced section; press. Cut two 30½ x 3-inch strips. Stitch strips to top and bottom of pieced section; press.

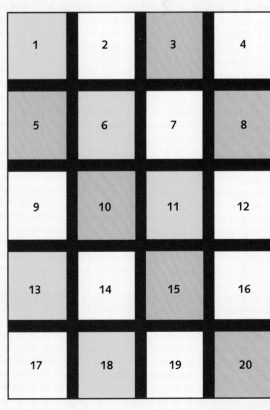

Diagram A

Photo A

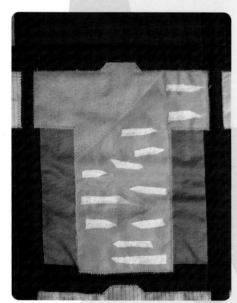

Photo B

5. Prepare template on page 102 **(see Transferring Patterns, page 5)**. Pin kimono template to selected fabric, trace around shape with marking pen or pencil, and cut along marked line. From striped gold silk, cut six kimonos. Pin or baste kimonos to squares 1, 8, 9, 14, 16, and 18 **(see Pinning and Basting, page 5)**. (*Note:* Kimonos will overlap seams slightly.) Adjust sewing machine to narrow zigzag with about 22 stitches per inch. With tan thread, zigzag over edges of kimonos. Trim loose threads.

6. From gold silk, cut five kimonos, Pin or baste kimonos to squares 2, 7, 11, 17, and 20. Zigzag over edges of kimonos. Trim loose threads.

7. From gold moiré, cut one kimono. Pin or baste kimono to square 5. Zigzag over edge of kimono. Trim loose threads.

8. From lavender fabric, cut three kimonos. Pin or baste kimonos to squares 4, 10, and 15. With lavender thread, zigzag over edges of kimonos. Trim loose threads. Remove pins or basting.

9. From green organza, cut 6 x 7-inch rectangle. Place five red petals on kimono in square 4. Place organza over kimono and pin in place at corners. Adjust machine to straight stitch and, using lavender thread, stitch on diagonal line and on zigzag stitching. (*Note:* Diagonal line is indicated on kimono template.) Also stitch intersecting random lines that enclose petals and divide space. Trim organza to within $\frac{1}{8}$ inch of seam. Also carefully trim organza from selected stitched areas **(see Photo A)**.

10. From green organza, cut 6 x 7-inch rectangle. From cream fabric, cut twelve irregular confetti strips measuring $\frac{1}{4}$ to $\frac{3}{8}$ inch long and $\frac{3}{4}$ to $1\frac{3}{4}$ inches wide. Place them on kimono in square 10. Place organza over kimono and pin in place at corners. Using lavender thread, stitch on diagonal line and on zigzag stitching. With cream thread, stitch over top of strips. When starting and stopping, reverse direction for two or three stitches to prevent unraveling. Trim organza to within $\frac{1}{8}$ inch of seam. Also carefully trim organza between selected confetti strips.

11. Repeat step 10 for kimono in square 15 **(see Photo B)**.

12. From white organza, cut twelve 6 x 7-inch rectangles. Place either flower petals or purple confetti strips on remaining kimonos **(see photo of finished project for placement)**. Refer to steps 9 and 10 to complete kimonos.

13. With wrong side up, place backing fabric on work surface. Carefully smooth out folds and center batting on top of backing fabric. With right side up, center quilt top on quilt batting.

14. Baste through all layers with pins or long basting stitches. Machine quilt as desired **(see Machine Quilting, page 6)**. Remove pins or basting. Trim thread ends. Trim edge of quilt. Stitch facing to quilt **(see Facing, page 7)**.

Kite Quilt

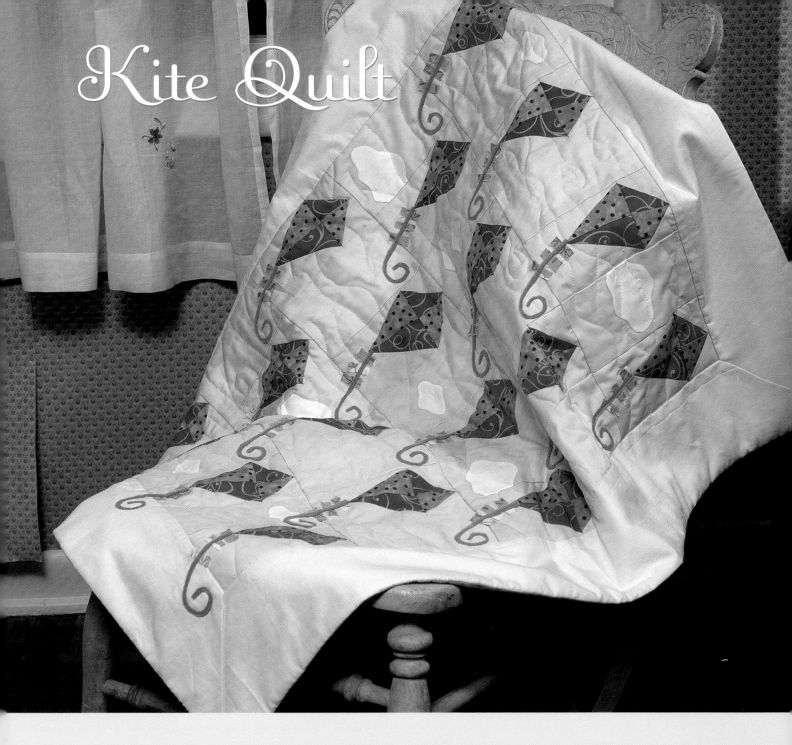

Transparent collage creates fabric windows that frame individual white clouds. Layered felt is used to make the kite tails.

Materials

¼ yard lavender print cotton

¼ yard purple print cotton

1 yard light blue cotton

¼ yard white cotton

¾ yard white silk organza

1¼ yards light peach cotton

⅛ yard peach print cotton

¾ yard blue felt

White and blue thread

34 x 41-inch piece of
cotton for backing

33 x 40-inch piece of batting

¾ yard cotton fabric
for facing

Marking pen or pencil

Black pencil

Fabric glue

FINISHED SIZE
32 x 39 inches

1. Prepare templates on page 102 **(see Transferring Patterns, page 5)**. Pin triangle templates to selected fabrics, trace around shapes with marking pen or pencil, and cut along marked lines. From lavender fabric, cut one A triangle and one B triangle. Reverse template and from purple fabric, cut one A triangle and one B triangle. From light blue fabric cut one of each of the C, D, E, and F shapes. Stitch together to make kite rectangle **(see Diagram A)**, stitching D shape on last; press. Repeat for total of eighteen kite rectangles.

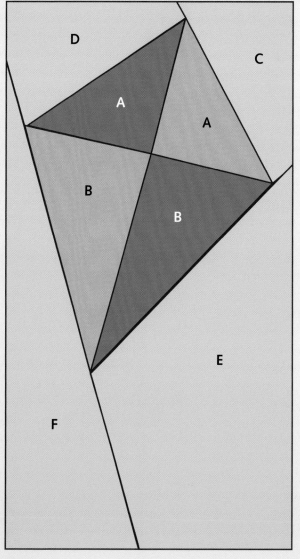

Diagram A

2. Pin cloud templates to white fabric, trace around shapes with marking pen or pencil; cut along marked lines. Cut five large clouds and seven small clouds. From organza, cut 4-inch square. Pin cloud to organza square. With white thread, stitch around outside edge of cloud; remove pins **(see Hand-Appliqué Shapes, page 77)**. Trim around seam line to within ⅛ inch of stitching. Cut notches in seam allowance at curves and corners. Cut 2-inch slit in organza. Turn right side out; press. Repeat with remaining clouds.

3. From blue fabric, cut seventeen 3¾ x 6½-inch rectangles. Place clouds on selected rectangles. (Large clouds are cropped in side seams.) From organza, cut seventeen 3¾ x 6½-inch rectangles. Layer organza on blue rectangles. Pin through all layers.

4. Alternating each, stitch kite rectangles to layered rectangles to make grid of seven across and five down; press.

5. From light peach fabric, cut two 5 x 35-inch strips and two 5 x 43-inch strips. Center short strips along top and bottom of quilt top and stitch, starting and stopping ¼ inch from each edge. Center long strips along sides and stitch, starting and stopping ¼ inch from each edge. Miter corners **(see Mitered Corners, page 6)**; press.

6. With black pencil, draw kite tails **(see page 105)** on wrong side of quilt top.

7. From peach print, cut eighteen ⅜ x 2-inch strips. Place small dot of glue on wrong side of each strip. adhere three strips below each kite **(see Photo A)**.

8. From blue felt, cut 3½ x 4½-inch rectangle. Place felt on work surface. Place quilt top, wrong side up, on felt. Center one kite tail on felt and pin at corners. With blue thread, stitch on marked line **(see the introduction to "Felt Layering," page 9)**; remove pins.

9. On right side of quilt top, carefully trim around kite tail. Trim peach strips to 1 inch wide. Repeat for remaining kite tails.

10. With wrong side up, place backing fabric on work surface. Carefully smooth out folds and center batting on top of backing fabric. With right side up, center quilt top on quilt batting.

11. Baste through all layers with pins or long basting stitches. Machine quilt as desired **(see Machine Quilting, page 6)**. Be sure to catch each cloud in quilting stitches. Remove pins or basting. Trim edge of quilt. Stitch facing to quilt **(see Facing, page 7)**.

Photo A

Paper Inspirations

Ever since paper was invented it has been used as an art medium and fashioned into colorful pictures and banners. Snipping paper has been popular for centuries and various cultures have developed distinctive styles. Cut-paper valances decorated peasant homes in Poland. A government official, Etienne de Silhouette, lent his name to French paper cutting because he amused himself at parties by snipping profiles of the guests. China and Japan also claim paper cutting as an important part of their artistic heritage. As with lace making, paper cutting creates textures and images through the play between positive and negative spaces.

This chapter features two different styles, German and Mexican paper cutting, which have been adapted for appliqué and rendered in fabrics of various colors and textures. The German technique, *scherenschnitte* ("scissors cutting"), became popular in America in the early 1800s when it was introduced by German and Swiss immigrants. Worked with a small pair of pointed scissors, the pieces were created one at a time from sturdy, solid-colored paper. Traditional German paper cuts often depicted rural scenes in intricate detail, even representing individual blades of grass. They sometimes included lacy hearts and geometric shapes within the composition, or in a decorative border. These works of art served as birth and marriage certificates and as fanciful valentines. If you come from a family of collectors, odds are there is a scherenschnitte valentine tucked away in an old shoebox in your attic.

The Mexican version is *papel picade,* ("punched paper"). Rather than cutting each piece separately, as many as fifty sheets of paper are layered and cut with a small chisel and a hammer. Multiple paper cuts are strung together and hung as banners at religious and civic celebrations. Since the pieces are done en masse, this look is larger, more graphic, and more stylized than the German interpretation.. Mexican designs are characterized by a paper grid that surrounds a central image. Paper appendages that would fall forward when hung, such as arms or wings, are anchored to the border by narrow lines. Common themes are saints, nativity scenes, birds, and animals. Tissue paper is preferred because of its delicate and ephemeral quality. While traveling, keep your eye out for churchyards or roadways festooned with cut-paper banners, and then prepare to join the party.

Since cut-paper designs are too intricate to execute with needle-turned or iron-on appliqué, two alternate techniques are used: layering or stabilizing. The Secret Garden Square, Hot Pursuit Dresser Scarf, and Silhouette Gift Bags use the layered technique, while the Swan Pillow uses the stabilizing method. The Mission Quilt combines both techniques.

Basic Instructions: Layering Technique

1. Cut the design from the fabric **(see Photo A)**.

2. Place the cut design on a contrasting background fabric **(see Photo B)**.

Photo B

Photo A

Photo C

Photo D

3. Layer organza over the design area **(see Photo C)**.

4. To secure, machine-stitch through two layers (the backing fabric and the organza) with an outline stitch around the design **(see Photo D)**. Finished projects that will be handled, such as throw pillows or gift bags, should be secured by this method because layers may shift with movement. Alternately, secure by machine-stitching three layers (the background fabric, the cut design, and the organza) into the construction seams of the project.

The five-step stabilizing technique requires lightweight, water-soluble stabilizer such as Solvy.™

Basic Instructions: Stabilizing Technique

1. Cut the design from the fabric **(see Photo E)**.

2. Place the cut design on a contrasting background fabric **(see Photo F)**.

3. Layer the stabilizer over the design area **(see Photo G)**.

4. Machine-stitch through three layers (the background fabric, the cut design, and the stabilizer) to secure the design **(see Photo H)**.

5. Following manufacturer's directions, immerse piece in water to dissolve stabilizer **(see Photo I)**.

The machine stitching can consist of a narrow zigzag, or a straight stitch that is carefully guided on the edge of he cut design. Or the stitching can be random and freeform and catch the outside edge of the cut design within an irregular stitching pattern. Unlike the layering technique, this technique requires stitching on rather than around the cut design to secure it to the background fabric.

Photo E

Photo F

Photo G

Helpful Hints

❋ Choose sharp scissors with a pointed end. In order to achieve accurate and detailed cuts, the cutting is done with the tips of the scissors rather than near the hinge.

❋ Before cutting, use many pins to anchor the template to the fabric. The design may become distorted if the template shifts while cutting.

❋ The raw edges of the cut fabric are neither turned under nor fused to webbing. The edges should be carefully trimmed, but it is almost impossible to prevent or remove all stray threads. Consider the imperfections a part of the artistry.

Photo I

Photo H

Swan Pillow

With the crude grid behind the central image, this pillow has the feel of *papel picade,* the Mexican cut-paper technique. The slits that articulate the swan's wing and those that highlight the water look as if they could have been cut with a blunt chisel. Enjoy the irregularities of the raw edges as an interesting design element.

Materials

⅓ yard light blue cotton

⅓ yard dark teal cotton

⅛ yard russet cotton

1 yard light toile fabric

10½-inch square water soluble stabilizer

16-inch square pillow form

White thread

FINISHED SIZE
18 x 18 inches

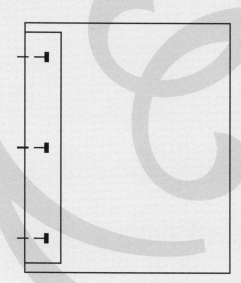

Diagram A

1. Prepare template on page 103 **(see Transferring Patterns, page 5)**.

2. From light blue fabric, cut 10½ x 9-inch rectangle. Center template on rectangle, pin in place, and cut out negative areas. It is important to cut accurately, so don't rush this step.

3. From teal fabric, cut 10½ x 9-inch rectangle. Center swan rectangle on teal rectangle. Carefully trim and remove any jagged edges or loose threads. Place stabilizer square over swan square. Pin or baste through all layers **(see Pinning and Basting, page 5)**.

4. Adjust sewing machine to zigzag with about 16 stitches per inch. Carefully stitch on light blue fabric along edge of swan. When starting and stopping, reverse direction of stitching for two to three stitches to prevent unraveling. Adjust sewing machine to straight stitch with about 13 stitches per inch. Stitch on light blue fabric on edges of grid lines, on waves, on beak, and on swan body to form wing **(see Photo A)**. Remove pins or basting stitches.

5. Following manufacturer's directions, immerse piece in water to dissolve stabilizer. Let dry; press. Trim loose threads. Since block may shrink slightly, trim to 10 x 8½ inches.

Photo A

6. From russet fabric, cut two 10 x 1¼-inch strips. Stitch strips to top and bottom of swan block; press. From toile fabric, cut four 3¾ x 13-inch strips. Stitch strips to swan block; press.

7. From toile fabric, cut four 2¾ x 16½-inch strips. With right sides together, fold one strip in half lengthwise. Stitch short sides together. Trim excess fabric from corners and turn right side out; press. Repeat with remaining strips. Matching raw edges, pin strips to pillow top **(see Diagram A)**.

8. From toile fabric, cut 16½-inch square. With right sides together, pin square to pillow top. Stitch together, leaving 10-inch opening along one side. Remove pins. Trim excess fabric at corners. Turn right side out; press. Insert pillow form. Hand-stitch opening closed.

Secret Garden Square

This project stays true to traditional *scherenschnitte,* with children playing in a quaint setting. Silhouettes are charming because they portray movement and gesture with a mere outline. The sheer layer relies on the slightly matte finish of silk organza, which here is preferable to the sheen of polyester. Although silk organza is more opaque than synthetic versions, the design shows well behind it.

Materials

½ yard black cotton

½ yard white cotton

½ yard white silk organza

½ yard floral print fabric

White thread

Marking pencil

Premade frame, 14 inches square

Picture mat to fit frame, with 9½-inch square window

FINISHED SIZE

15 inches square

1. Prepare template on page 104 **(see Transferring Patterns, page 5)**.

2. From black fabric, cut 12-inch square. Center template on black square, pin in place, and carefully cut out negative areas. It is important to cut accurately, so don't rush this step.

3. From white fabric, cut 12-inch square. Center cut square on white square. Carefully trim and remove any jagged edges or loose threads.

4. From organza, cut 12-inch square. Place organza over design area. Pin or baste through all layers **(see Pinning and Basting, page 5)**.

5. Adjust sewing machine to straight stitch with about 13 stitches per inch. Carefully stitch around design. When starting and stopping, reverse direction of stitching for two to three stitches to prevent unraveling. Stitch on white fabric as closely as possible to black fabric. (Machine stitches will hold threads of cut edge in place.) Do not stitch on black fabric. After outlining, fill in white areas with continuous random stitching. Trim thread ends. Remove pins or basting stitches.

6. With marking pencil, draw 8½-inch square, centered on back of square, for seam lines. Trim to within ¼ inch of marked lines.

7. From floral fabric, cut four 3 x 11¼-inch strips. Stitch strips to square **(see Log Cabin Border, page 5)**; press.

8. Insert square into mat and frame. If you prefer, have the piece professionally stretched and framed.

Hot Pursuit Dresser Scarf

Early poets declared February 14 the official day of love, since that was considered the day that both birds and men choose their mates. An entire industry of expressing affection sprung up with lacy paper valentines. This *scherenschnitte* design was inspired by historical valentines to tell the story of unrequited love.

Materials

¼ yard black cotton

¼ yard white cotton

¼ yard white silk organza

1 yard floral print fabric

1 yard rayon fringe in coordinating color

White thread

Thread to match floral print

Marking pencil

FINISHED SIZE

14¼ x 40 inches

1. Prepare template on page 105 **(see Transferring Patterns, page 5)**.

2. From black fabric, cut 15¼ x 7½-inch rectangle. Center template on black rectangle, pin in place, and carefully cut out design. It is important to cut accurately, so don't rush this step.

3. From white fabric, cut 15¼ x 7½-inch rectangle. Center cut design on white rectangle. Carefully trim and remove any jagged edges or loose threads.

4. From organza, cut 15¼ x 7½-inch rectangle. Place organza over design area. Pin or baste through all layers **(see Pinning and Basting, page 5)**.

5. Adjust sewing machine to straight stitch with about 13 stitches per inch. Using white thread, carefully stitch around design. When starting and stopping, reverse direction of stitching for two to three stitches to prevent unraveling. Stitch on white fabric as closely as possible to black fabric. (Machine stitches will hold threads of cut edge in place.) Do not stitch on black fabric. After outlining, fill in white areas with continuous random stitching. Trim thread ends. Remove pins or basting stitches.

6. With marking pencil, draw 14¼ x 6½-inch rectangle, centered on back of design rectangle, for seam lines. Trim to within ¼ inch of marked lines.

7. From floral fabric, cut 14¾ x 1½-inch strip. Stitch strip to bottom of design rectangle; press. Cut 14¾ x 33-inch rectangle. Stitch rectangle to top of design rectangle; press.

8. From fringe, cut two 14¾-inch lengths. Pin or baste bound edge of one strand of fringe to one end of scarf with fringe pointing toward center of scarf. Turn ends of fringe out at corners **(see Diagram A)**. Repeat with second length of fringe on opposite end of scarf.

9. From floral fabric, cut 14¾ x 40½-inch rectangle. With right sides together, pin rectangle to scarf top. Stitch together leaving 5-inch opening along one side; remove pins. Trim excess fabric from corners. Turn right side out; press. Hand-stitch opening closed.

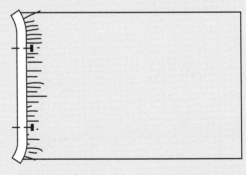

Diagram A

Silhouette Gift Bags

Borrow the cupid and the suitor from the dresser scarf to make a special *scherenschnitte*-style gift bag. A pleat in the bottom of the bag adds roominess.

Cupid Gift Bag

Borrow the cupid from the dresser scarf to make a special *scherenschnitte*-style gift bag for a special gift. A pleat in the bottom of the bag adds roominess.

Materials

6 x 6-inch square black fabric.

¼ yard white silk organza

⅓ yard light weight metallic fabric

½ yard rayon cord or ribbon

White thread

Air-soluble marking pen

FINISHED SIZE
10¼ x 13 inches

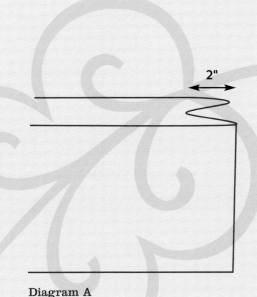

Diagram A

1. Prepare template **(see Transferring Patterns, page 5)**, using only cupid and bow from Hot Pursuit Dresser Scarf template **(page 105)**.

2. Center design on black square, pin in place, and carefully cut out design. It is important to cut accurately, so don't rush this step.

3. From organza, cut two 8-inch squares. Center cut design on one square. Place second square on top and pin or baste through all layers **(see Pinning and Basting, page 5.)**

4. Adjust sewing machine to straight stitch with about 13 stitches per inch. Carefully stitch around design. When starting and stopping, reverse direction of stitching for two to three stitches to prevent unraveling. Stitch on organza as closely as possible to black fabric **(see Photo A)**. (Machine stitches will hold threads of cut edge in place.) Do not stitch on black fabric. Trim thread ends. Remove pins or basting stitches. With water-soluble pen, draw 6-inch square on organza, centered around design.

5. Trim metallic fabric to 10¾ x 42 inches. Pin design square 9½ inches from one short side of rectangle, centered between the two longer edges. Adjust sewing machine to a zigzag stitch with about 11 stitches per inch. Machine-stitch along marked line, securing design square to fabric. Trim thread ends.

6. With wrong sides together, fold rectangle in half, width-wise. Fold in opposite direction with a 2-inch pleat at original fold line **(see Diagram A)**.

Photo A

7. Adjust sewing machine to a straight stitch. Starting 7 inches from top of bag, stitch sides together. Cut seams to starting point **(see Diagram B)**. Turn right side out. Starting at top of bag, stitch to previous seams **(see Diagram C)**; press.

8. Fold top edge down twice to create a cuff.

9. Insert gift. Tie bag below cuff with cord or ribbon.

Diagram B
Begin seam 7" from bag top. Cut horizontal slit in seam allowance at starting point. Do not cut through stitching.

Diagram C
Fold right side out, then stitch top 7" of seam to starting point in Diagram B.

Valentine Postman Gift Bag

Materials

6 x 6-inch square black fabric.

¼ yard white silk organza

⅓ yard lightweight metallic fabric

½ yard rayon cord or ribbon

White thread

Air-soluble marking pen

FINISHED SIZE
10¼ x 13 inches

Desperate for that perfect gift bag? Make this attractive *scherenschnitte* bag and add new meaning to the phrase "Special Delivery."

⟨◦⟩

1. Prepare template **(see Transferring Patterns, page 5)**, using only man and heart from Hot Pursuit Dresser Scarf template **(page 105)**.

2. Complete steps 2 through 9 of Cupid Gift Bag.

Mission Quilt

During the late 1800s, the Mission style emerged as a counterbalance to the florid ornamentation of the Victorians, with emphasis on simplicity and comfort rather than embellishment and formality. This quilt was designed in the manner of Mission textiles.

Mission interiors took themes and colors from nature, hence the serene colors and the stark animal and botanical silhouettes. The overall design consists of one combination of blocks turned and repeated. This is the only project in this chapter made with polyester organza rather than silk organza. Since polyester organza is shinier, it makes a good contrast to the matte tones of the cottons. Choose a very sheer polyester organza with just a slight tint of green.

Materials

1¾ yards gray cotton

1¼ yards dark brown cotton

½ yard avocado green cotton

¼ yard gold cotton

¼ yard light green cotton

¼ yard light green polyester organza

¼ yard dull pink cotton

¼ yard chartreuse print cotton

1¼ yard water soluble stabilizer

45 x 57-inch piece of batting

46 x 58-inch piece of cotton fabric for backing

5¼ yards double-fold bias binding

Dark brown thread

FINISHED SIZE
43 x 55 inches

1. From gray fabric, cut two 4 x 57-inch and two 4 x 45-inch strips for border. Set aside.

2. Prepare templates on pages 106–7 for squirrel, rabbit, and branch with berries **(see Transferring Patterns, page 5)**.

3. From dark brown fabric, cut twelve 7-inch squares. Center rabbit template on one brown square, pin in place, and cut out negative areas. It is important to cut accurately, so don't rush this step. Repeat with remaining squares.

4. From avocado fabric, cut twelve 7-inch squares. Center one cut rabbit square on one avocado square. Carefully trim and remove any jagged edges or loose threads. From stabilizer, cut twelve 7-inch squares. Place one square of stabilizer over rabbit square. Pin or baste through all layers **(see Pinning and Basting, page 5)**.

5. Adjust sewing machine to a narrow zigzag stitch with about 22 stitches per inch. Carefully stitch on brown fabric along edge of design. When starting and stopping, reverse direction of stitching for two to three stitches to prevent unraveling. Repeat with remaining squares. Remove pins or basting stitches.

6. From dark brown fabric, cut twelve 6½ x 5½-inch rectangles. From gold fabric, cut twelve 6½ x 5½-inch rectangles. Repeat steps 3 through 5 to make squirrel blocks. (*Note:* Squirrel blocks have no border around design.)

7. Following manufacturer's directions, immerse rabbit and squirrel blocks in water to dissolve stabilizer. Let dry; press. Trim any loose threads.

8. From dark brown fabric, cut twelve $4\frac{1}{2}$ x $6\frac{3}{4}$-inch rectangles. Center branch template on one brown rectangle, pin in place, and cut out negative areas. Repeat with remaining rectangles.

9. From light green fabric, cut twelve $4\frac{1}{2}$ x $6\frac{3}{4}$-inch rectangles. Center one cut branch rectangle on one light green rectangle. Carefully trim and remove any jagged edges or loose threads. From organza, cut twelve $4\frac{1}{2}$ x $6\frac{3}{4}$-inch rectangles.

10. Place one organza rectangle over one branch rectangle. Pin or baste through all layers. Adjust sewing machine to straight stitch with about 13 stitches per inch. Carefully stitch around design. When starting and stopping, reverse direction of stitching for two to three stitches to prevent unraveling. Stitch on organza as closely as possible to brown fabric. (Machine stitches will hold threads of cut edge in place.) Do not stitch on brown fabric. Trim thread ends. Remove pins or basting stitches. Repeat for remaining rectangles.

11. Since rabbit and squirrel blocks may shrink slightly, trim rabbit blocks to $6\frac{3}{4}$-inch squares and squirrel blocks to 6 x $5\frac{1}{4}$ inches. From dull pink fabric, cut twelve 6 x 2-inch strips. From chartreuse print, cut twelve $3\frac{1}{4}$ x $6\frac{3}{4}$-inch rectangles. From gray fabric, cut twelve $4\frac{3}{4}$ x $6\frac{3}{4}$-inch rectangles, and twelve $6\frac{3}{4}$ x $2\frac{3}{4}$-inch rectangles. Using one of each, stitch together to make one combined block **(see Diagram A)**; press. Repeat for total of twelve combined blocks.

12. Stitch together combined blocks **(see Diagram B)**; press.

13. Center short strips from step 1 along top and bottom edges of quilt top and stitch, starting and stopping $\frac{1}{4}$ inch from each edge. Center long strips along side edges and stitch, starting and stopping $\frac{1}{4}$ inch from each edge. Miter corners **(see Mitered Corners, page 6)**; press.

14. With wrong side up, place backing fabric on work surface. Carefully smooth out folds and center batting on top of backing fabric. With right side up, center quilt top on quilt batting.

15. Baste through all layers with pins or long basting stitches. Machine quilt as desired **(see Machine Quilting, page 6)**. Remove pins or basting. Trim thread ends. Trim edge of quilt. Stitch bias binding around edge of quilt **(see Binding, page 6)**.

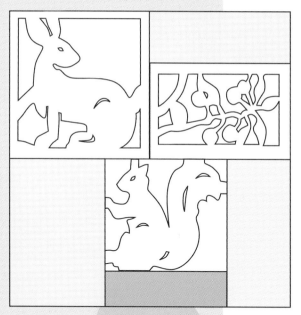

Diagram A

Diagram B

Unreal Chenille

Chenille has a long history. Marie Antoinette used an early version of this technique to embellish silk clothing, cutting through rows of tiny satin stitches to add fuzzy accents to sleeves and collars. (In fact, the word *chenille* means "caterpillar" in French.) The chenille that we know today has come a long way from the fuzzy bathrobes and tufted bedspreads that were the comfort fibers of the 1950s, to become a sophisticated choice for everything from carpet to upholstery. And now with chenille appliqué, you can add interesting three-dimensional shapes to your fiber projects.

C henille appliqué brings the process full circle, from small accents to large textured fields, back to small accents. The marked area is filled with parallel rows of machine-stitched fabric, trimmed to create a design shape, and then cut into rows to create texture. The images are defined by a filled texture, so simple graphic shapes work best. Create interest by changing the direction of the stitching of neighboring shapes, and by using several prints and/or colors of fabric in one design. Choose matte cotton, soft flannel, or brushed rayon velvet.

Basic Instructions

1. Draw the design on the wrong side of the fabric **(see Photo A)**.

2. Layer the backing fabric on the appliqué fabric. Projects featuring rayon velvet require one layer of velvet; those featuring cotton need two layers of cotton. The template indicates the direction of the stitching lines. Rotate the appliqué fabric if necessary so the lines are diagonal to the fabric grain. Stitch the rows on the fabric bias to prevent unraveling.

3. Machine stitch parallel lines in the design areas, spacing the rows ⅜ to ¼ inch apart **(see Photo B)**. When starting and stopping a row, reverse the direction for two or three stitches to prevent unraveling.

4. Trim around the design shape **(see Photo C)**.

5. Cut between the stitched rows **(see Photo D)**.

Helpful Hints

✳ Since the design is marked on the wrong side of the fabric, a number 2 pencil or colored pencil can be used. But if you want the lines to disappear, use an air-soluble marking pen.

✳ If the design is not symmetrical, reverse the template before marking the fabric.

✳ When cutting out the design shape, cut close to the stitching, being careful not to cut through the backing fabric. When cutting between the stitched rows, make small even cuts using small scissors with a sharp point. Don't use a seam ripper because it's too easy to cut through the background fabric. Fluff up the cut edges by rubbing them with your fingers or with a terrycloth towel.

✳ When beginning a project, measure and mark the stitching lines on one or two sections. After filling in a section or two, you can judge the correct space between the lines, using the width of the presser foot as a guide.

Photo A

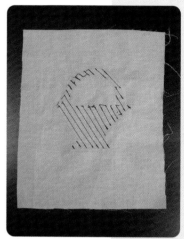

Photo B

Photo C

Photo D

Thistle and Wreath Quilt

This large thistle print is the perfect complement to the soft wreath shapes. If a thistle print is not available, choose a large-scale floral or topiary print. This piece can be used as a baby quilt, a doll quilt, or a tablecloth.

Materials

1 yard thistle-print fabric

¼ yard green rayon velvet

½ yard lavender print fabric

⅛ yard blue cotton

1½ yards light blue print fabric

45 x 45-inch piece of cotton for backing

44 x 44-inch piece of batting

5 yards double-fold bias binding

Green thread

Tracing paper

Marking pen or pencil

FINISHED SIZE
42 x 42 inches

1. On a photocopier, enlarge one leaf from **Diagram A** at 275%.

2. From thistle fabric, cut 11-inch square. Draw 3½-inch-diameter circle, centered on wrong side of square. Draw leaves around marked circle **(see Diagram A)**.

3. From green velvet, cut 3-inch square on bias. Place square on work surface, wrong side up. Center one marked leaf from step 2 on square. Pin in place at corners. Noting direction, stitch parallel lines within design area **(see page 77, step 3)**. Trim thread ends; remove pins.

4. On right side of fabric, trim around shape. Cut between parallel lines. Trim end of each row to a right angle.

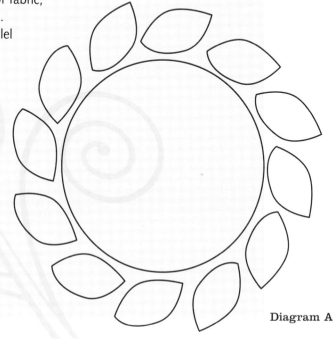

Diagram A

Photo A

5. Repeat steps 3 and 4 for remaining leaves to complete wreath **(see Photo A)**.

6. Repeat Steps 2 through 5 to make a total of five appliquéd squares.

7. From lavender fabric, cut 4½-inch square and four 3¾-inch squares. From thistle print, cut four 4½ x 3¾-inch rectangles. Stitch squares and rectangles together **(see Diagram B)**; press. Repeat for total of four pieced squares.

8. Stitch appliquéd squares to pieced squares, alternating to make checkerboard-style grid of three across and three down; press.

9. From blue fabric, cut four 1¼ x 34-inch strips. Stitch strips around the four sides of pieced section, starting and stopping ¼ inch from each edge. Miter corners **(see Mitered Corners, page 6)**; press.

10. From light blue print, cut four 5 x 44-inch strips. Stitch strips around the four sides of pieced section, starting and stopping ¼ inch from each edge. Miter corners; press.

11. Place backing fabric on work surface, wrong side up. Carefully smooth out folds and center batting on top of backing fabric. Center quilt top on quilt batting, right side up.

12. Baste through all layers with pins or long basting stitches **(see Pinning and Basting, page 5)**. Machine quilt as desired **(see Machine Quilting, page 6)**. Remove pins or basting. Trim threads. Trim edge of quilt. Stitch bias binding around edge of quilt **(see Binding, page 6)**.

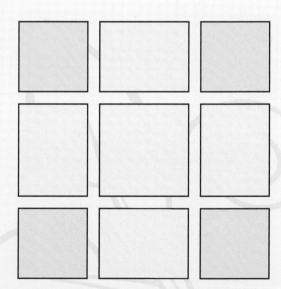

Diagram B

Starry Night Quilt

A sky full of playful three-dimensional stars serves as a dreamy backdrop for this row of sleepy houses. Each star is divided into four sections of tufted fabric. Tipping the stars within the pieced squares seems to make them dance.

Materials

1 yard dark blue print cotton

¼ yard yellow print cotton

¼ yard light gold cotton

¼ yard medium gold cotton

⅓ yard light blue print cotton

⅛ yard burgundy cotton

⅛ yard rust print cotton

1½ yards teal print fabric

¼ yard lavender cotton

¼ yard gray print cotton

¼ yard dark red cotton

¼ yard chartreuse print cotton

Scraps of rust, light blue, olive, and black cotton

36 x 48-inch piece of cotton for backing

35 x 47-inch piece of batting

1⅓ yards dark blue cotton for facing

Yellow and black thread

Marking pen or pencil

FINISHED SIZE

33 x 45 inches

1. Prepare templates on page 107–8 **(see Transferring Patterns, page 5)**.

2. From dark blue fabric, cut 6-inch square. Draw star design, centered on wrong side of square **(see photo of finished project for placement)**.

3. From yellow print, cut two 3 x 3½-inch rectangles on bias. Layer rectangles and place, wrong side up, on work surface. Center top section of star on rectangles. Pin in place at corners. Noting direction and using yellow thread, stitch parallel lines within design area **(see page 77, step 3)**. Trim thread ends; remove pins. On right side of fabric, trim around shape. Cut between parallel lines **(see Photo A)**.

4. Repeat Steps 2 through 4 to fill remaining three sections of star. Use light gold fabric for side sections and medium gold for bottom sections.

5. Repeat Steps 2 through 5 to make a total of eight appliquéd squares. Square end of each row by trimming perpendicular to stitching line.

6. From light blue print, cut four 1½ x 7-inch strips. Stitch strips to an appliquéd square to make a log cabin border **(see Log Cabin Border, page 5)**; press. Repeat for remaining squares. Draw seam lines on wrong sides of squares **(see Diagram A)**. Trim to within ¼ inch of marked lines.

7. From dark blue print, cut eight 7-inch squares. Alternating plain squares and appliquéd squares, stitch together to make checkerboard-style grid of four across and four down; press.

Photo A

8. Pin house templates to selected fabrics, trace around shapes with marking pen or pencil, and cut along marked lines. Cut five house shapes, one each of gray print, dark red, and chartreuse print, and two of lavender; and cut five elongated triangles, one each of light blue, burgundy, and olive, and two of rust **(see Photo B for color orientation)**.

9. Stitch long sides of triangles to left sides of house shapes; press. Starting ¼ inch from top edges of seams, stitch houses together. From dark blue print, cut six triangles for sky immediately above houses. Stitch sky triangles to houses, stopping ¼ inch from corners **(see Diagram B)**; press. Trim side triangles flush with raw edges of house strip.

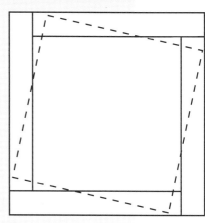

Diagram A

10. Stitch house strip to bottom of star grid; press. On wrong side of houses, mark windows and chimneys, referring to templates for placement. From black fabric, cut 1½ x 3½-inch rectangle. Place rectangle on work surface and center one marked chimney on rectangle. With black thread, stitch along marked lines. Trim threads. On right side of quilt top, trim around chimney. Repeat for remaining chimneys and windows.

11. From rust print, cut 26½ x 3½-inch strip. Stitch strip to bottom of house strip; press.

12. From burgundy fabric, cut two 1¼ x 38-inch strips. Stitch strips to sides of pieced section; press. Cut two 28 x ½-inch burgundy strips. Stitch strips to top and bottom of pieced section; press.

Photo B

13. From teal print, cut 28 x 4-inch strip. Stitch strip to top of pieced section; press. Cut two 44½ x 4-inch teal print strips. Stitch strips to sides of pieced section; press. Cut one 35 x 4-inch teal print strip. Stitch strip to bottom of pieced section; press.

14. With wrong side up, place backing fabric on work surface. Carefully smooth out folds and center batting on top of backing fabric. With right side up, center quilt top on quilt batting.

15. Baste through all layers with pins or long basting stitches **(see Pinning and Basting, page 5)**. Machine quilt as desired, following quilting template on page 109 **(see Machine Quilting, page 6)**. Remove pins or basting. Trim threads. Trim edge of quilt. Stitch facing to quilt **(see Facing, page 7)**.

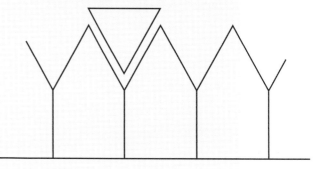

Diagram B

Good Night Pillow

Unreal chenille pairs with felt layering to add pizzazz to this pillow. The center square and border strips are cut from the same fabric, but the square is wrong side up, achieving a change in value without altering the fabric hue.

Materials

½ yard dark blue print cotton

Scraps of cream, pink print, and yellow cotton

Scraps of cream, pink, and black felt

6-inch square white polyester organza

⅛ yard medium blue felt

⅓ yard medium blue print cotton

12-inch pillow form

Pink, blue, cream, and black thread

Air-soluble marking pen

Marking pencil

FINISHED SIZE

12 inches square

1. From dark blue print, cut 7½-inch square, 7½ x 1¾-inch strip, 7½ x 4¼-inch strip, 3¾ x 12½-inch strip, and 2¼ x 12-inch strip. Stitch square and strips together **(see Diagram A)**; press. (*Note:* Be sure to assemble with the square wrong side up for subtle value change.)

2. Prepare templates on page 110 **(see Transferring Patterns, page 5)**. Pin templates to selected fabrics and trace around shapes with marking pen. From cream fabric, cut moon. From yellow fabric, cut shadow shape. Aligning bottom edges, place shadow shape on moon. Stitch along broken line. With right sides together, pin moon to organza square. Stitch around outside edge; remove pins. Trim around seam line to within ⅛ inch of stitching. Cut notches in seam allowance at curves and corners **(see Diagram B)**. Cut a 2-inch slit in organza. Turn right side out and press.

3. Stitch moon to center square **(see photo of finished project for placement)**. With marking pencil on wrong side of square, draw the details: eye, eyebrow, cheek, lip, script, and star.

4. From pink fabric, cut two 2¾-inch squares. Layer squares and place wrong side up on work surface. Place pillow top, wrong side up, on squares. Center cheek on squares; pin at corners. Using pink thread and noting direction, stitch parallel lines within circle **(see page 77, step 3)**; remove pins. On right side of square, trim around circle. Cut between parallel lines.

5. From blue felt, cut 6 x 4-inch rectangle. Place felt on work surface. Place pillow top, wrong side up, on felt. Center "good" on felt and pin at corners. With blue thread, stitch on marked line **(see introduction to "Felt Layering," page 9)**; remove pins. On right side of square, trim around script.

6. Using matching threads, stitch and trim "night," star, lip, eye, and eyebrow.

7. From medium blue print, cut 12½-inch square. With right sides together, pin square to pillow top. Stitch together, leaving 6-inch opening along one side; remove pins. Trim excess fabric from corners. Turn right side out. Insert pillow form. Hand-stitch opening closed.

Diagram B

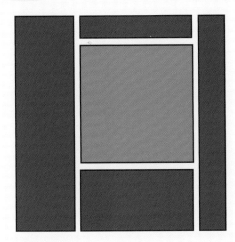

Diagram A

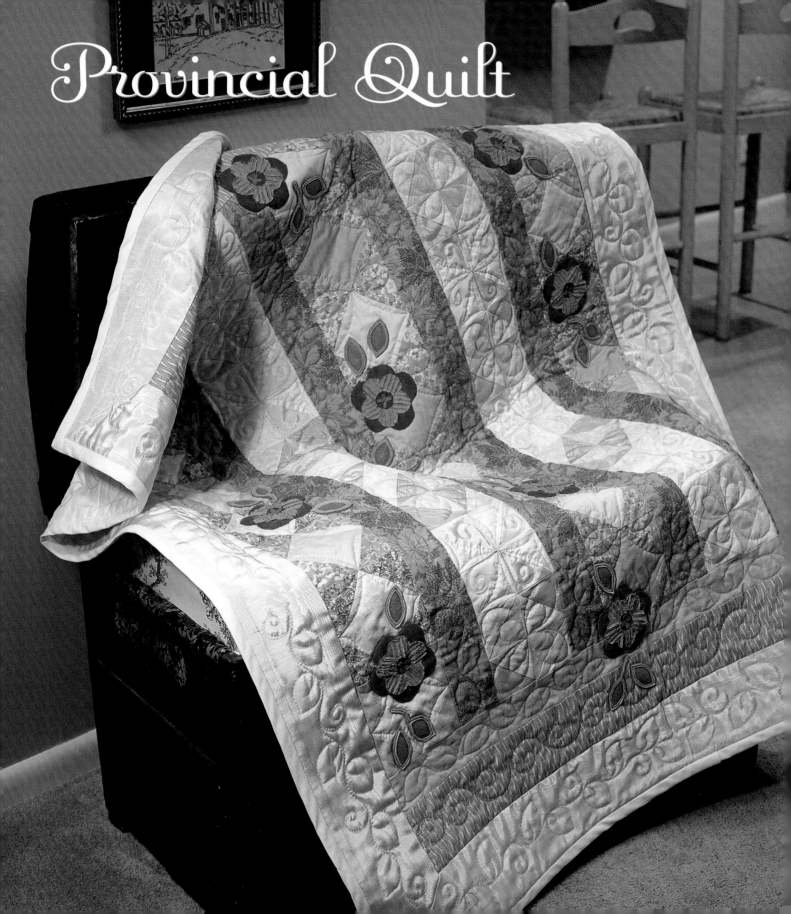

Provincial Quilt

Materials

2 yards pink moiré fabric

Assorted peach print cottons (floral, paisley, leaf print, etc.)

Assorted lavender cottons (light solid, medium solid, print, etc.)

¼ yard cream print fabric

¼ yard gold moiré fabric

¼ yard lavender print fabric

⅓ yard periwinkle print cotton

⅛ yard green cotton

¼ adobe print fabric

¼ yard burgundy fabric for flowers

¼ yard violet fabric for flower centers

¼ yard white silk organza

⅓ yard medium green felt

⅓ yard light green felt

44 x 58-inch piece of cotton for backing

43½ x 57½-inch piece of batting

5½ yard double-fold bias binding

Purple and green thread

Marking pen or pencil

Black pencil

FINISHED SIZE

42 x 56 inches

Provincial walls and furniture are often embellished with faded flowers and then sanded to add age and character. The chenille flowers on this quilt suggest the worn look of provincial country decorating. The flowers combine unreal chenille with felt layering.

———

1. From pink moiré, cut two 5 x 46-inch and two 5 x 60-inch strips for border. Set aside.

2. Prepare templates on pages 106–7 **(see Transferring Patterns, page 5)**.

3. Pin triangle template to one peach print, trace around shape with marking pen or pencil, and cut along marked line. Cut three more triangles. From a lavender fabric, cut 4-inch square. Stitch together to make one square **(see Diagram A)**. From different combinations of peach and lavender, make total of twenty-four squares; press.

4. Stitch eight squares together to make one vertical strip; press. Repeat for total of three strips.

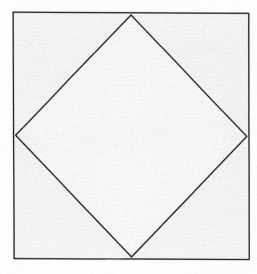

Diagram A

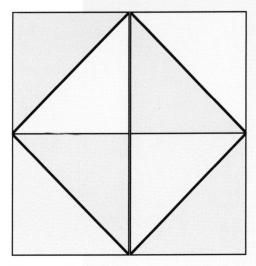

Diagram B

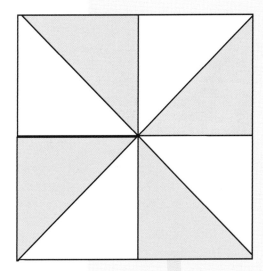

Diagram C

5. From pink moiré, cut four triangles. From cream print, cut four triangles. Stitch together to make one square **(see Diagram B)**; press. Repeat for total of eight squares.

6. From gold moiré, cut four triangles. From lavender print, cut four triangles. Stitch together to make one square **(see Diagram C)**; press. Repeat for total of eight squares.

7. Alternate four B squares and four C squares to make a vertical strip; press Repeat to make second strip.

8. From periwinkle fabric, cut four 2¾ x 40½-inch strips. Stitch between pieced strips **(see Diagram D)**; press.

9. From green fabric, cut 2½ x 34½-inch strip. Stitch strip to bottom of pieced section; press. From adobe fabric, cut two 3½ x 34½-inch strips. Stitch strips to top and bottom of pieced section; press.

10. Center short strips from step 1 along top and bottom of quilt center. Stitch, starting and stopping ¼ inch from each edge. Center long strips along sides of quilt center. Stitch, starting and stopping ¼ inch from each edge. Miter corners **(see Mitered Corners, page 6)**; press.

11. Pin larger flower template to burgundy fabric, trace around shape with marking pen or pencil, and cut along marked line. From organza, cut 5-inch square. With right sides together, pin flower to organza square. Stitch around outside edge; remove pins. Trim around seam line to within ⅛ inch of stitching. Cut notches in seam allowance at curves and corners. Cut 2-inch slit in organza. Turn right side out, press **(see Hand-Appliqué Shapes, page 7)**. Repeat for total of ten flowers.

12. With pencil and smaller flower template, draw inner flowers and Xs on wrong sides of flowers.

13. From violet fabric, cut two 4½-inch squares. Layer squares and place on work surface. Place one flower, wrong side up, on squares. Pin in place around edges. Using purple thread and noting direction, stitch parallel lines within inner flower **(see page 77, step 3)**; remove pins. On right side of flower, trim around and inside inner flower. Cut between parallel lines. Repeat for remaining flowers.

14. From medium green felt, cut 1½-inch square. Place felt on work surface. Place one flower wrong side up on felt, centering X on felt. With green thread, stitch along marked line **(see introduction to "Felt Layering," page 9)**. On right side of flower, trim around X. Repeat for remaining flowers.

15. Arranging flowers in random pattern, hand-stitch flowers to quilt top. With pencil, draw leaves on wrong side of quilt top.

16. From light green felt, cut 4-inch square. From medium green felt, cut 4-inch square. On work surface, layer felt squares with medium green square on top. Place quilt top, wrong side up, on squares. Center one leaf section (two leaves or two leaves and one stem) on squares and pin at corners. With green thread, stitch on marked line **(see page 77, step 3)**; remove pins.

17. On right side of quilt top, trim both layers of felt from around leaves. Carefully trim light green felt from inside leaves to reveal medium green felt. Repeat for remaining leaf sections and single leaves.

18. With wrong side up, place backing fabric on work surface. Carefully smooth out folds and center batting on top of backing fabric. With right side up, center quilt top on quilt batting.

19. Baste through all layers with pins or long basting stitches. Machine quilt as desired **(see Machine Quilting, page 6)**. Remove pins or basting. Trim edge of quilt. Stitch bias binding around edge of quilt **(see Binding, page 6)**.

Diagram D

Templates

All templates are shown at full size, unless otherwise noted. When templates need to be scaled larger, enlarge them on a photocopy machine at the specified percentage.

CROCODILE PILLOW, page 14 (enlarge 130%)

NEST PILLOW, page 12 (enlarge 110%)

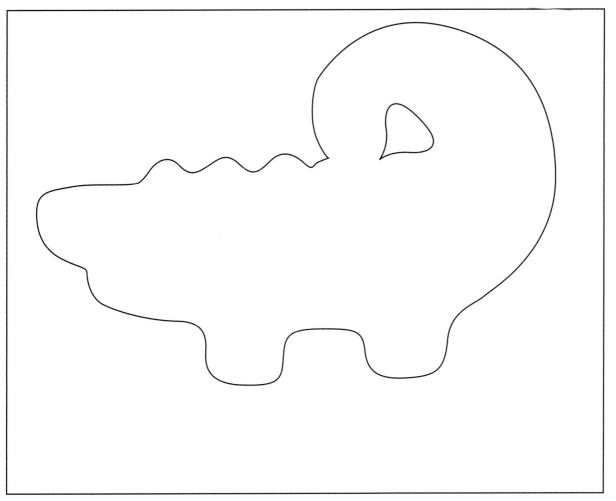

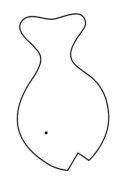

CROCODILE PILLOW, page 14

CROCODILE PILLOW, page 14

PAPER HEART PILLOW, page 26

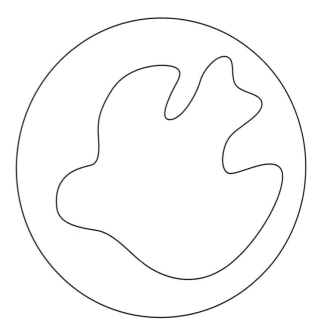

BIRD AND BERRIES PILLOW, page 34

BIRD QUILT, page 18

Template A

Template B

Template C

Template D

Template E

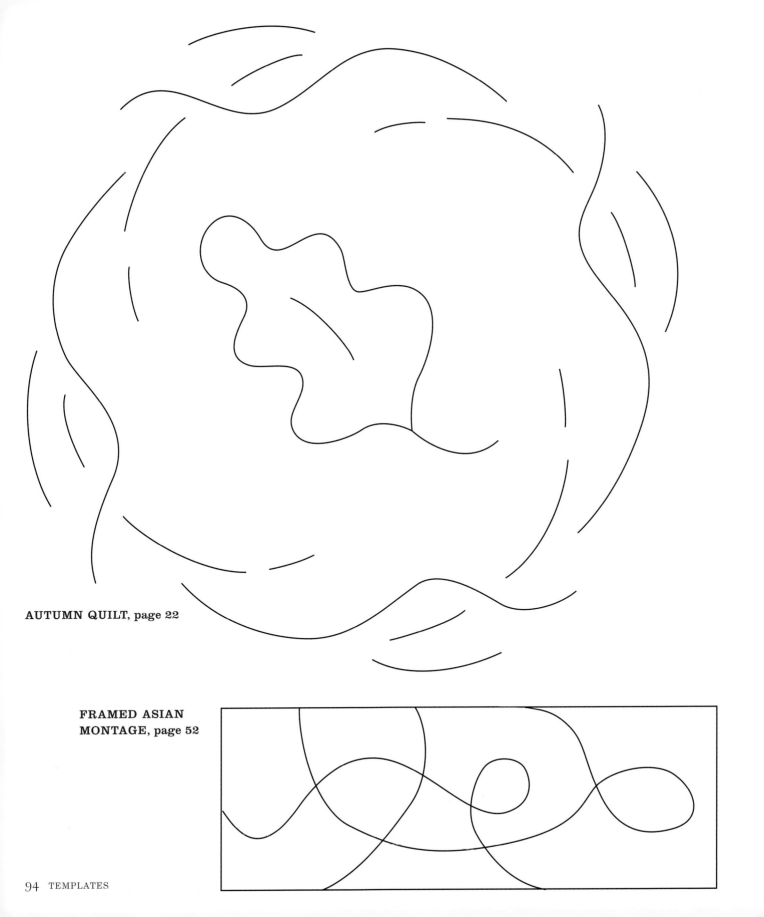

AUTUMN QUILT, page 22

FRAMED ASIAN MONTAGE, page 52

ACORN PILLOW, page 24 (enlarge 135%)

FRAMED ASIAN
MONTAGE, page 52

ACORN PILLOW, page 24

FRAMED ASIAN MONTAGE, page 52

FISH PILLOW, page 16 (enlarge 120%)

SKELETON KEY PILLOW, page 30 (enlarge 110%)

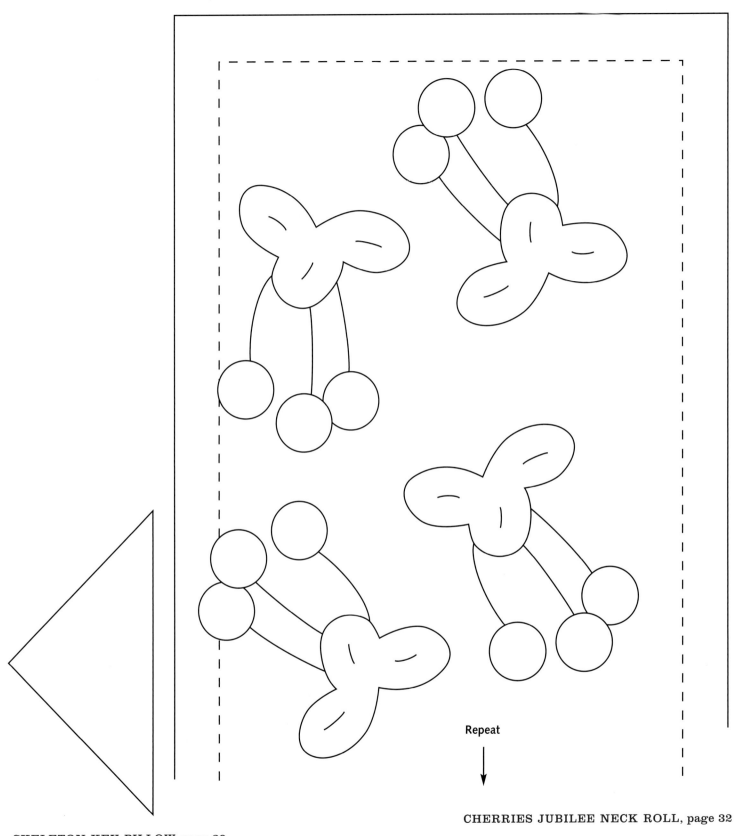

Repeat

CHERRIES JUBILEE NECK ROLL, page 32

SKELETON KEY PILLOW, page 30

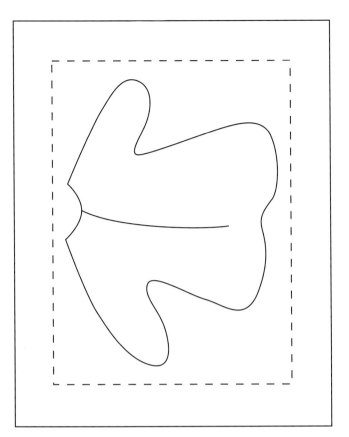

Template A

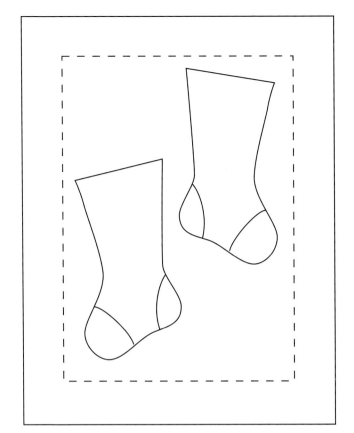

Template B

THANK-A-SHEEP QUILT,
page 36 (enlarge 115%)

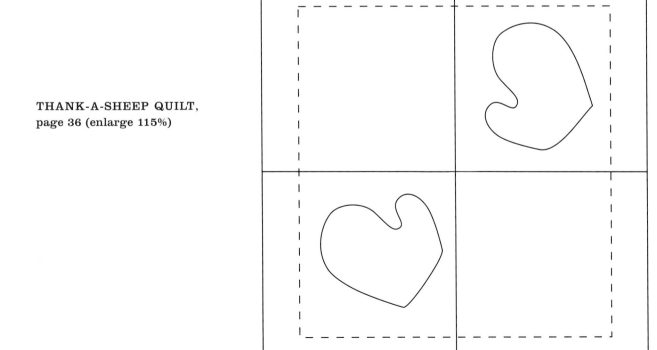

Template C

THANK-A-SHEEP QUILT, page 36: Template D (actual size)

EIFFEL TOWER PILLOW, page 49

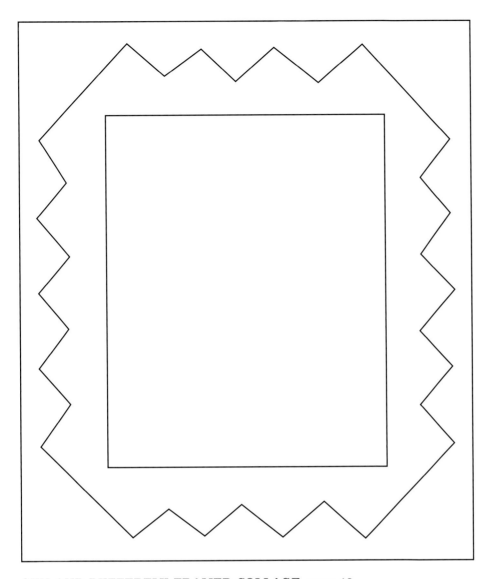

SUN AND BUTTERFLY FRAMED COLLAGE, page 46

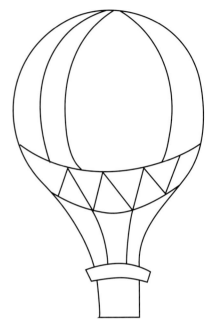

HOT-AIR BALLOON
PILLOW, page 51

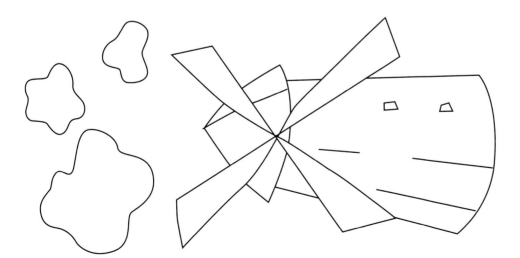

WINDMILL PILLOW, page 50

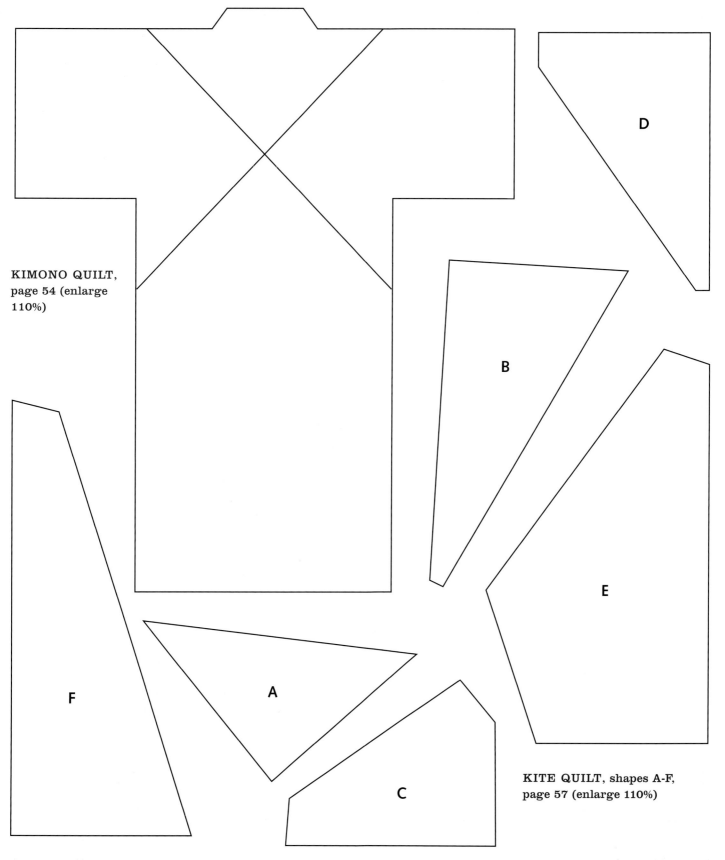

KIMONO QUILT,
page 54 (enlarge
110%)

KITE QUILT, shapes A-F,
page 57 (enlarge 110%)

SWAN PILLOW, page 64

SECRET GARDEN SQUARE, page 66

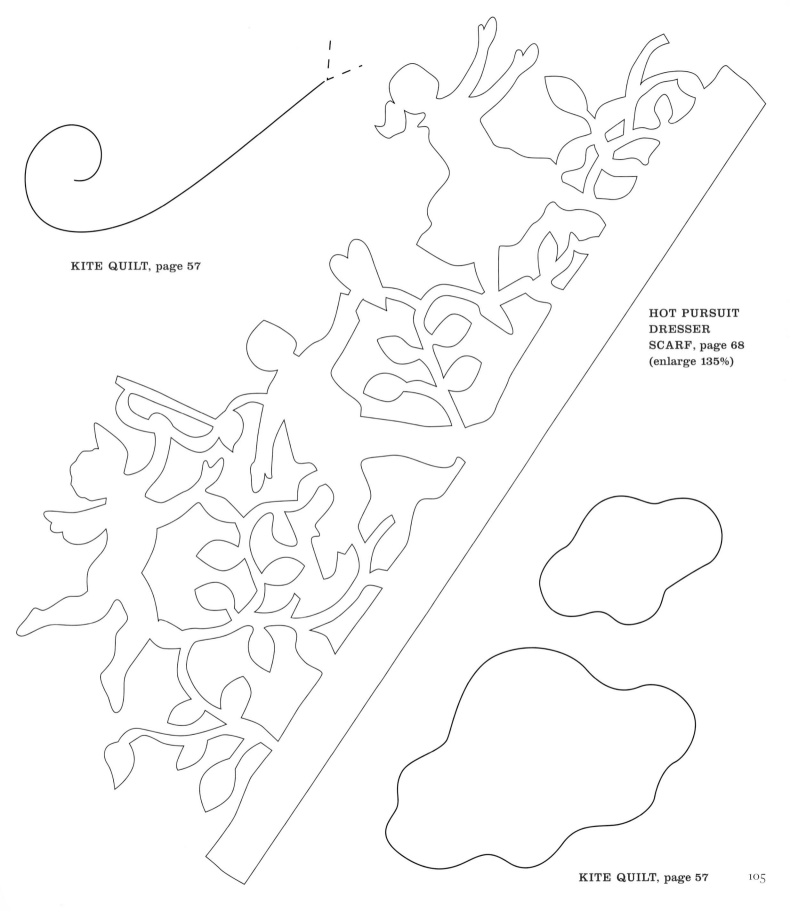

KITE QUILT, page 57

**HOT PURSUIT
DRESSER
SCARF,** page 68
(enlarge 135%)

KITE QUILT, page 57

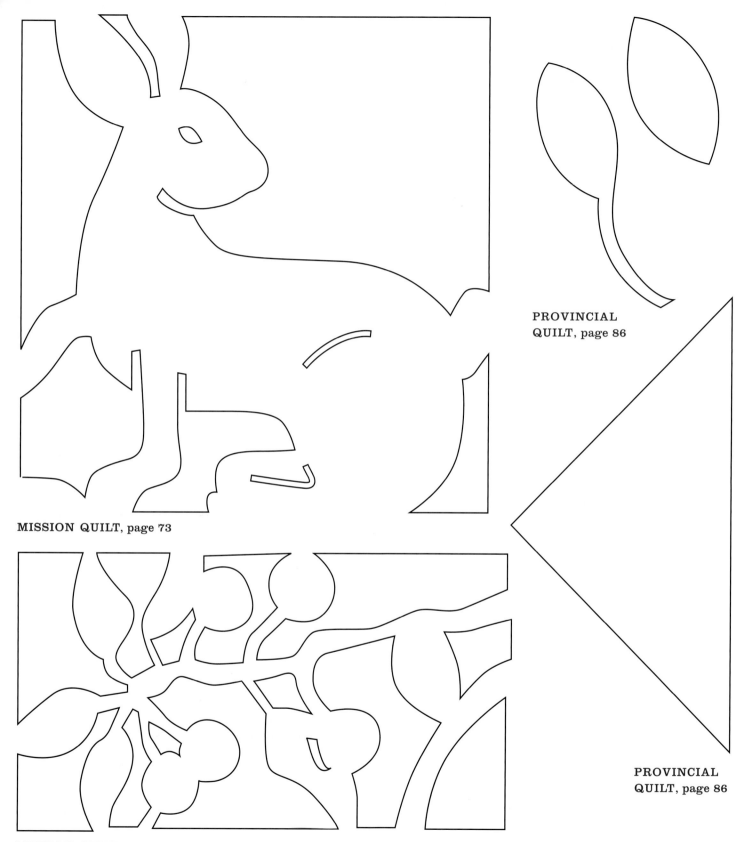

PROVINCIAL
QUILT, page 86

MISSION QUILT, page 73

PROVINCIAL
QUILT, page 86

MISSION QUILT, page 73

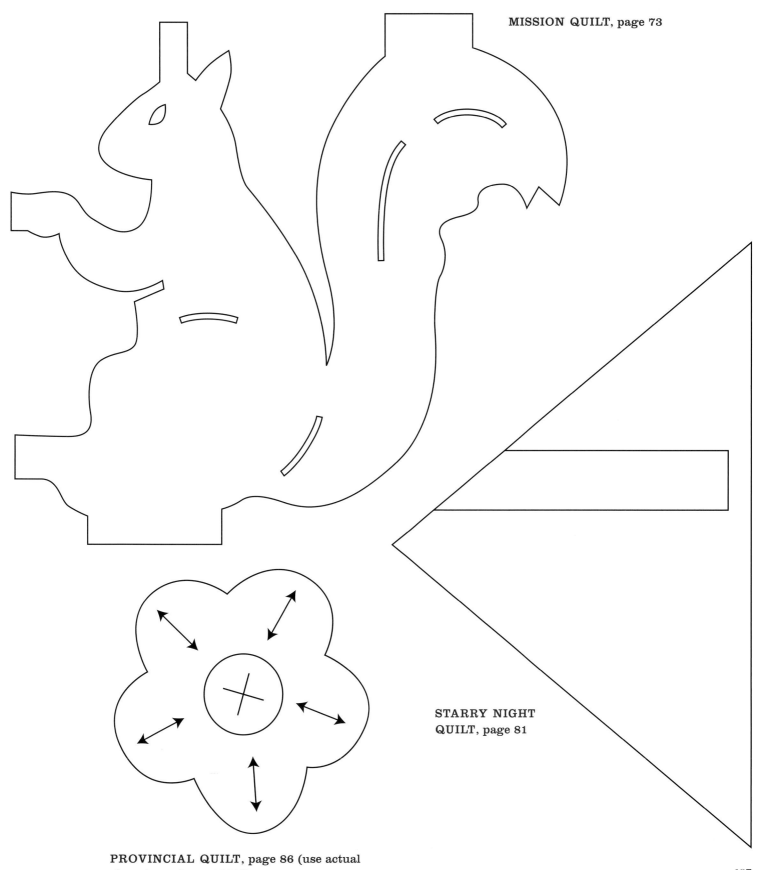

STARRY NIGHT
QUILT, page 81

PROVINCIAL QUILT, page 86 (use actual
size; also enlarge 135%)

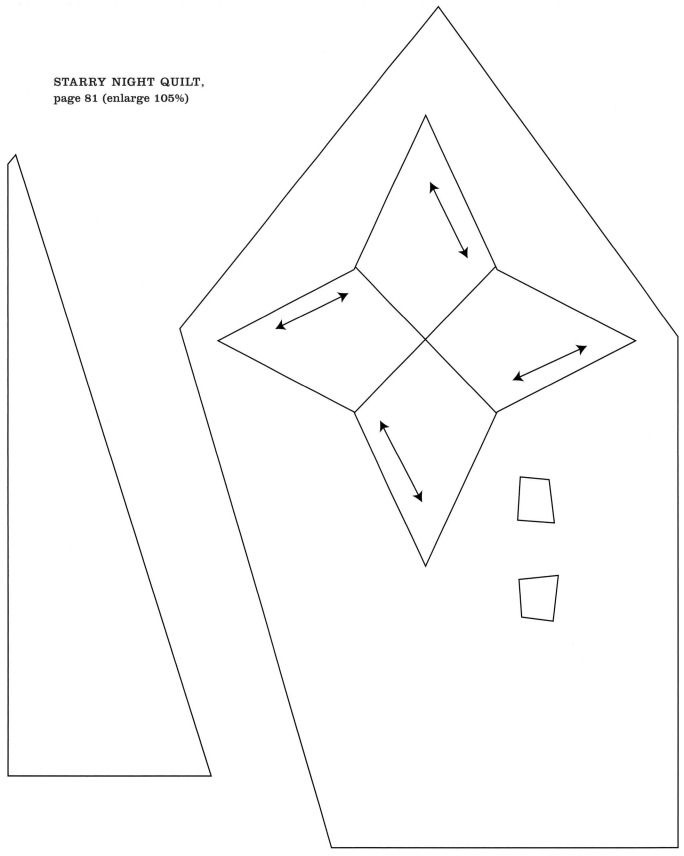

STARRY NIGHT QUILT, page 81: quilting template

**GOOD NIGHT
PILLOW, page 84**

good
night

Sources

Most supplies for the projects in this book are readily available at local fabric and craft stores. For further information on products, consult the websites of the manufacturers listed here.

Coats & Clark

www.coatsandclark.com

Yarn, thread

Crescent

www.crescentcardboard.com

Mat board

DMC

www.dmc-usa.com

Embroidery floss

Duncan Enterprises

www.duncancrafts.com

Fabric glue

Fairfield Processing Corp.

www.poly-fil.com

Fiberfill

Fiskars Brands Inc.

www.fiskars.com

Scissors

Halcraft USA Inc.

www.halcraft.com

Beads

Kunin Felt

www.kuninfelt.com

Felt

Morning Glory Products

www.carpenter.com

Batting

National Nonwovens

www.nationalnonwovens.com

Felt

Plaid Enterprises

www.plaidonline.com

Acrylic paint

Prym Dritz

www.dritz.com

Sewing notions, air-soluble marking pen

Ranger Industries

www.rangerink.com

Ink pads

Rubber Stampede, Inc.

www.rubberstampede.com

Rubber stamps

Sanford Corporation

www.sanfordcorp.com

Colored pencils

Sulky of America Inc.

www.sulky.com

Water-soluble stabilizer

Therm O Web

www.thermoweb.com

Double-sided adhesive

Index